RE-SCRIPT YOUR LIFE

Reeta Gupta is one of India's most sought after content specialists and human rights evangelists. Her team at The Network, delivers influencer-led, content-based campaigns in both traditional and social media.

She has worked for programmes of the Government of India, the global disability sector, several charitable foundations as well as private sector organizations in healthcare, e-commerce and education. With a passion for the English language since her childhood, Reeta believes that 'saying it in a few words' is her specialty. She prefers to spend all her free time with her family.

Story-telling to yourself can change the perception you have about yourself. As an athlete I have used this tool many times even in pressure situations to make myself do things I didn't think I was capable of. You need to 'will' yourself. The mind is an endless ocean of vast reserves. It's up to you to find yourself and rescript your life.

—*World No. 1 shooter Heena Sidhu*

There are so many voices in our heads all the time, it is so important to find the voice of your true north and follow that even amid the endless chatter. Your internal monologue plays a large role in your mental health let the universe lead the way!

—*Miss Malini, celebrity blogger, entrepreneur*

Rescript Your Life is a book that lays out a simple 5-point plan to change the way you speak to yourself and therefore, your experience of life. Kindness within is kindness without. Reeta Gupta reminds us that our strongest enemy lives in between our ears.

—*Dr Swaroop Sampat Rawal, educator, actor*

Let go of the fear that you are inadequate in any way. Embrace all of you and make the most of the opportunities you get. Encourage the tiny, inner sparks of potential within you so they grow into the fervour of fulfilment.

—*Deepa Malik, 2016 Rio paralympics silver medalist, Arjuna Awardee*

RE-SCRIPT YOUR LIFE

Awaken the Voice Within You

REETA GUPTA

Published by
Rupa Publications India Pvt. Ltd 2018
7/16, Ansari Road, Daryaganj
New Delhi 110002

Sales centres:
Allahabad Bengaluru Chennai
Hyderabad Jaipur Kathmandu
Kolkata Mumbai

Copyright © Reeta Gupta 2018

The views and opinions expressed in this book are the author own and the facts are as reported by her which have been verified to the extent possible, and the publishers are not in any way liable for the same.

All rights reserved.
No part of this publication may be reproduced, transmitted, or stored in a retrieval system, in any form or by any means, electronic, mechanical, photocopying, recording or otherwise, without the prior permission of the publisher.

ISBN: 978-93-5304-071-0

First impression 2018

10 9 8 7 6 5 4 3 2 1

The moral right of the author has been asserted.

This book is sold subject to the condition that it shall not, by way of trade or otherwise, be lent, resold, hired out, or otherwise circulated, without the publisher's prior consent, in any form of binding or cover other than that in which it is published.

*I dedicate the book to my friends Dheeraj, Neeha and Karan,
who have filled me with a lifetime of happiness.*

This book is dedicated to my country, India, which provided a democratic, peaceful, environment to me as I was growing up. I realize that to many of my fellow citizens of the world, even a peaceful walk, two square meals a day or a day in school not interrupted by terrorism is a dream. The law and order in my country gave me the freedom to educate myself, explore my talents and express my convictions.

I also dedicate this book to the genius philosophers of our country and to their works that are still accessible and revered all over the world.

Lastly, a note of gratitude for my mothers. My biological mother who ensured my upbringing and education, and created opportunities in my life, and to my mother-in-law who showed me how human compassion can come to your rescue in situations where logic and education both fail.

Contents

Foreword by Col Rajyavardhan Rathore, AVSM (Retd)   *xv*
Prologue   *xvii*
Preface   *xxi*

Rescripting Your Life—the Why

1. Your Self-concept   3
2. Your Worst Enemy Could Be You   5
3. What Makes You the Way You Are?   8
4. Here's Why Motivation Is Short-lived   11
5. Small Talk And a Lifetime Of Limitations   16
6. Reprogramme Your Internal Monologue   19
7. Why Do We Put Off Self-improvement For Another Day?   23
8. Unshackling the Chains Of Habit   27
9. The Spiritual Way To Tame the Monster In Your Head   30

Rescripting Your Life—the How

10. Stage 1: Connect To Your Source   35
11. Stage 2: Opt Out Of Being Ordinary (Embracing THECO)   44
12. Stage 3: Activate Your Imagination   79

13. Stage 4: Master Your Emotions — 95
14. Stage 5: Find Your Values — 113

In Conclusion

15. Awaken the Voice Within You — 139

Epilogue — 145

Bibliography — 147

My everyday mantra:
Even on your worst day, don't stop loving yourself.

For centuries, your greatest enemy has lived between your ears. It is now time that it became your greatest friend.
This book is your practical guide to a progressive mind and a peaceable life.

*The one who loves all intensely
begins perceiving in all living beings
a part of himself.
He becomes a lover of all,
a part and parcel of the universal joy.
He flows with the stream of happiness,
and is enriched by each soul.*

YAJUR VEDA

What you listen from others is what your ears hear. That's external appreciation, criticism or validation. But the most powerful conversation happens between your ears, in your mind. You can hear that conversation louder than any other. That's internal self-worth.
You are only as good as your next thought about yourself.

Foreword

This book encourages every youngster, to look within, and change the conversation around what it means and what it takes to be a success.

Often, we make the mistake of focussing our self-image on external appreciation. It is nobody's job to shine the spotlight on us, but our own.

Your self-worth is your spotlight.

Because the story you tell yourself, has to go beyond labels that are given to you. You can achieve greater heights, when you compete with the best within you, and become your own coach.

Let's celebrate everyone, our teachers, our farmers, our musicians, the folks doing routine jobs in public service offices. Be kind, in word and deep spread the universal power of peace and appreciation.

Col Rajyavardhan Rathore, AVSM (Retd)

Minister of State (I/C) for Youth Affairs
and Sports, Minister of State for
Information and Broadcasting (I/C), and
silver medallist at the 2004 Olympics

May 2018

Prologue

26 December 2016: The Day I Almost Died.

We were on the Mumbai–Ahmednagar expressway, en route to a military training camp of the Armoured Corps Centre. Three children and two adults in a car.

It was 11 p.m. and finally, after a long journey, we were barely 20 km away. Two trucks stopped ahead of us. It all seemed normal.

Suddenly, the truck in front of us reversed aggressively and hit the bonnet of our car with full force.

Boom! What followed is unimaginable. The truck pushed against us, dragging us for almost a kilometre in reverse along a straight path, with brute force. The momentum was crazy and the children were terrified. The youngest started crying loudly.

In what now seems impossible, almost a divine act in some way, we somehow managed to swerve out of the uncontrollable backward force and violently did a reverse U-turn, getting out of the truck's way. The crazy truck driver soon banged hard against the divider in the middle of the road and overturned.

By some inexplicable luck, there were no cars behind us. And without divine intervention, our car would've been up in flames that night. My whole family could have been obliterated.

When we swerved out of what seemed like an eternity of being pushed back, with no control over the next moment, the full force of the gratitude we always forget to express hit me like a tight slap.

I realized that whatever life was given to me after this accident belonged to a higher power. It wasn't mine alone. Hence, I feel obligated to share my life lessons with the world.

This is no ordinary self-help book. Because you don't need help—you need a moment of truth that you experience for yourself.

This book is an exercise in self-belief, and a way out of the 'Am I Good Enough (AIGE)?' trap.

Part-autobiographical, this book is a quick read on how to take charge of your life and start treating yourself with respect.

Preface

Take a look around yourself.

Would you say that it's an ideal world? Certainly not. We could do with more equality of opportunities, peace and happiness.

The World Health Organization (WHO) says that between 2005 and 2017, depression (low self-concept) rose by more than 18 per cent worldwide.

What is depression?

One way to look at depression is 'a lack of mindfulness', and an unwillingness to accept your own present circumstances. Your mind is wandering some place, away from the now, and placing the expectation of happiness in that place, and yearning for it.

It is high time you stopped confusing a wandering mind with imagination. The 'power of imagination' is a positive force that can transform your future. Depression however, imagines the worst and acts on it too.

Let me tell you an open secret: from the moment you are born, every communication you have ever received is imprinted in your brain.

Everything you listen to, everything you talk about, everything you see, every action you take, every experience you have—and even every thought you have—leaves an imprint in your brain.

The more the repetition in the message you receive, the more it is imprinted in the wiring of your brain. You can call this your 'conditioning' or your 'programming'.

Think of a popular chart busting song. What is repeated more is remembered more. Every such song repeats a phrase that has your brain hooked, so that you remember it effortlessly. From A. R. Rahman's 'Jai ho' to Justin Bieber's 'Baby', the music industry knows this to be true.

The areas within your brain, which store messages, don't know to differentiate between bad or good, positive or negative. They offer mechanical storage of whatever is repeated often enough and act on it as if it's true.

Think of it this way; your smartphone learns to recognize words that you use repeatedly, and starts prompting the spelling without really knowing the meaning.

So even if you're typing 'hopeful', your smartphone will prompt 'hopeless' thanks to conditioning and repetition.

All of us are subject to this past conditioning.

A lifetime of negative messages, wired into your brain can be detrimental. You can be confused about who you are, and what your life's purpose.

At such times, you look for easy escapes from your situation. These include avoiding the difficult conversations in life as well as all the 'filters' that author and motivational speaker Simon Sinek has mentioned, filters which we put on ourselves to look engaged and 'happening' on the social media.

What we see around us, teenage suicides, a rise in depression, inability to cope, unemployment, lack of tolerance, religious conflict and even terrorism are a result of individuals, desperately trying to find an identity, and to 'belong somewhere', regardless of how 'low' or 'distorted' that place is.

Our young deserve better. You deserve better!

We need to work together to build a world, where parents know the consequences of their words and actions, and youngsters know how to seek positive experiences and reinforcements.

We can only create this world, by harbouring a peaceable mind and learning to value ourselves.

The following ancient Indian spiritual texts have been referred for this book:

All the four Vedas:

- Rig Veda
- Sama Veda
- Yajur Veda
- Atharva Veda

Other important texts include:

- The early Upanishads
- Brahma Sutra
- Mahabharata
- Bhagavad Gita
- Ramayana
- Puranas.

RESCRIPTING YOUR LIFE—THE WHY

1

Your Self-concept

How often have you heard these? Or said these.

- I have trust issues.
- I don't look good in that colour.
- I don't have time.
- How could I ever be happy with the circumstances that define my life?
- My father is a patient of depression.
- I can't focus!
- I feel that others don't respect me.
- I tend to give up easily.
- I always put my foot in my mouth!
- I never manage to be punctual.
- I don't feel confident about public speaking.
- I'm not talented, so I have to work harder than everyone else.
- I never get a break!
- I never get paid my due.
- I never get anything till it's too late.
- Lady luck and I walk on parallel roads.
- My divorced aunt lives with me; that's why my life is hell!

- I cannot control my drinking habit.
- I am in a hopeless situation.
- I'm always broke by the end of the month.
- My hair sucks!
- Interviews scare the living daylights out of me.
- I'm not very good on the phone.
- Today isn't my day!
- I just can't remember any names.
- I can't choose; you choose for me!
- All this motivation stuff is bullshit! Never works for me.
- I can never quit smoking; it's a very sticky habit.
- I used to have far more energy; now it's all downhill.
- I never know what to say at the right time.
- My brother is far more talented than I am.
- Mom always loved my sister more.

2

Your Worst Enemy Could Be You

There's a mental monologue you have with yourself all the time. You talk to yourself by force of habit. Unconsciously, you are reinforcing everything that is imprinted in your brain.

Your parents, teachers and other significant people in your life would have tried their best for you since your childhood. But they also may have undergone their share of 'negative experiences' imprinted on their brain, handed down from their own parents, friends and teachers. They too would have been preoccupied with their own internal negative monologues.

This negative 'wiring of thought' has prevented them from becoming and doing exactly what they wanted to do with their lives. And they transfer their disappointments and their experiences to you.

The good news is that creating a new wiring in your brain is up to you! You don't have to take every 'unflattering opinion' that is handed down to you.

Have you seen two brothers born from the same parents who have the same relatives and go to same school, experience the same environment very differently from each other when growing up? Because one brother's internal monologue is very different from the other's.

Any mental monologue that questions your capabilities, any nonsense you feed your mind, creates gaps between your expectations and your reality. And this is what causes stress and depression.

Did you know that an estimated 75 to 90 per cent of all doctor visits, all over the world, are due to stress-related issues? Yet, despite its high healthcare costs, depression continues to remain below the radar for policy-makers and health insurance companies. The reasons for this could be many:

1. Depression, like obesity, is thought to be no big deal. 'She'll be all right in a few days', or 'he needs to just sort himself out', is a normal response.
2. Depression is considered extremely personal, and what's worse, it is thought that one's mental problems have no effect on anyone else.
3. There has been no social or political movement to tackle depression as there has been to fight smoking or cancer.

My submission to you is that you have to stop being your own enemy!

To come out of this self-sabotage, you need more than theoretical knowledge. You have to 'action' what you read here in order to experience genuine transformation.

So if I were to tell you that 1. Science tells us that it is easier to recollect more recent events or messages than older ones, and 2. You can therefore always think a new thought and tell yourself something new and fulfilling, a genuine transformation does seem simple and doable.

Within you lies the immense potential to reverse negativity, optimize your future, focus on your plans and achieve the success that you were meant to have.

Think of it this way—if 'you' don't think, talk or feel good about yourself, or love yourself, why should anyone else?

The key lies in telling yourself the right things, which then reflect in a more assertive and confident you. Two interventions are outlined in this book—one at the internal level and the other at the external level.

Lasting, effective re-programming of your internal monologue is a deeply transformative process.

3

What Makes You the Way You Are?

Think of the last time you had to connect your TV to the internet, or to a sound system or a gaming system like PS4. You have to connect tonnes of wires of different diameters. And once you have set it up fully, even a minor glitch can be frustrating.

Can you imagine the amount of wiring in your brain?

The circumference of the earth is 40, 075 km. The total length of axons (the wires) in the human brain of a twenty-year-old is more than four times this length (1,76,000 km)!

However, the total length of wiring in a brain shrinks to 97, 200 km by the age of eighty—just two-and-a-half times the circumference of the earth.

Consider this—the thoughts and behaviour you are made up of are connected to this wiring in your brain, and this wiring clearly reduces with age.

The secret to the individual differences between any two people lies in the wiring of their brains.

Let's understand how.

How are we wired at birth?

According to work by the world's leading neuroscientists, variations in the way our brains develop before birth strongly influence us throughout our lives, shaping our personality, intelligence, sexuality and even the way we perceive the world.

We all share a genetic programme for creating a human brain. The programme for making your brain is specifically encoded in your DNA. As you developed in your mother's womb, the neurons (nerve cells) in your brain grew, and then discovered and connected with the different parts of your body. Every one of these countless connections must be attached precisely between the correct neurons in the brain to form functional circuits.

The sheer number of axons (wires remember?) that are required to connect 100 billion neurons into functional circuits will leave us flabbergasted!

This is what you are born with.

How does your brain develop after birth?

The good thing is your brain changes throughout your life, so you can rid yourself of some of your parental baggage! Every experience you have will impact the structure of your brain. The modern human brain is extensively shaped by the environment, and evolves as we learn, remember the meaning of our social connections and adapt to our surroundings.

Furthermore, looking at the brain's wiring through a scan reveals surprising patterns as per the Human Connectome Project. People with more 'positive' variables, such as more education, better physical endurance and above-average performance on memory tests, shared the same wiring patterns. Their brains seemed to be more strongly connected (held together) than those of people with 'negative' traits such as smoking, aggressive behaviour or a family history of alcohol abuse.

Consumption of drugs and alcoholism can pull the brain down into a negative spiral and damage some important connections. You can disturb the wiring of your brain if you frequently blame yourself when something bad happens; if you automatically anticipate the worst in a situation; if you put too much pressure on yourself (for example, you either have to be perfect or if you mess up once, you're a failure—no in-between); if you magnify the negative parts of a situation and dismiss the positive ones.

Your self-dialogue, or the unspoken words you tell yourself, combine your conscious thoughts with your unconscious beliefs and biases and cause imprints on the brain.

These imprints become stronger over time and can be retrieved from your brain, just like a file from a computer. These imprints, such as 'I am not good at public speaking', will come up when you are faced with a situation that involves the activity that you're apprehensive of. Such negativity can be unrealistic, even harmful, but we do it anyway.

Like it or not, everything you say to yourself matters. The inner critic isn't harmless. It limits you, cripples you and stops you from pursuing the life that you truly want to live.

It robs you of peace of mind and emotional well-being and, if left unchecked long enough, it can even lead to not being able to perform at your full potential, or worse, serious mental health problems like depression or anxiety.

So is motivation the answer?

4

Here's Why Motivation Is Short-lived

I am sure most of you have attended motivational talks. A typical set-up, is a large hall with a stage and theatre-style seating for its audience. Anxious listeners, sit spellbound as a powerful orator, a master magician paints a beautiful canvas and gives you a whole new grand vision of yourself!

The mantra could be as tempting as, 'You can be anything you want. A few simple steps, practised every day can take you to riches and fulfilment.'

Mesmerized, you take copious notes and feel the blood rushing through your veins.

I am 'here'. I can be 'there'! It's so easy! Why didn't I think of it myself?

For a couple of hours. Maybe, even a couple of days, or even during the course of a week-long programme, you have a spring in your step.

Most of the motivational speakers you will encounter in life are highly evolved, skilled, well-meaning people, extremely aware of the effect they have on people. In fact being persuasive, effective communicators is part of their core-skill set and their training. They encourage you to put your thinking cap on and evaluate the choices you have in life.

As you and your fellow listeners emerge from the auditorium, you tell yourself, 'From tomorrow, I will begin the day as a new person!'

That's your new resolve—to build a new you.

Unfortunately, any such external motivation programme is no more than a cup of tea. It can be intensely satisfying and give you energy for a couple of hours only.

But you will feel the need to have tea again.

Soon.

Am I saying don't attend these programmes? Absolutely not. But go with a complete understanding of how these programmes work against you.

And what you *need* to do, if they have to work for you.

Imagine that you come back from one such programme and resolve to build a whole new physiology and lose about 10 kg.

You chart out a plan and devise your routines.

You begin to tabulate the weight loss.

Day 1: 800 gm

Day 2: 600 gm

Day 3: 300 gm

Day 4: 100 gm

That looks disappointing!

And your body hurts. Surely, you can't be working that hard to lose a measly 100 gm!

Suddenly, the distance between 100 gm and 10 kg looks ominous.

Day 5: Skip exercise, leg hurts.

Day 6: I have to spend time with my kids, can't exercise today.

Day 7: I have to visit the salon, my hair is a mess!

Day 8: It's Sunday!

Day 9: The weight you lost in the first four days is back.

This can be very disheartening for you. And this is probably the reason why motivation programmes can work against you.

Because when you go home, you get back to the details, chores and distractions of everyday life.

You may not even be aware that there is a powerful internal mechanism at work that is trying to override the *fresh* inspiration you got from the speaker.

These are the chains of habit that have developed within you, over the years. What we call 'programming' or 'conditioning'.

The only way for this 'set programming' to survive is to overpower anything that even remotely suggests any change.

Slowly, your mind starts to tell you that you are not as capable as the motivational speaker on the stage thought you were.

You may have attended this motivation programme as a part of a sales team from a corporation, as an individual entrepreneur, or in a group of mixed people.

All of you may have been looking for some inspiration to fix stagnation, and reach new heights of achievement.

Your body then chips in, says that it's just too much effort.

One minor defeat—Day 5 of skipping exercise, leads to another, Day 6, when you suddenly remember you haven't spent quality time with your kids. Well, exercise with them, if that's your excuse!

By now, you are back in your comfort zone. Your ever

powerful habit-activated internal programming wins out. *Am I good enough?* you ask yourself.

Some of you will give up, at this point. Your mind is constantly telling you, that all this 'motivational bullshit' is for others, not for you! *I'm not made for all this* is how you deal with this.

A handful of you may realize exactly what your mind is making you do. And work on a simpler routine.

Instead of straightaway planning a 45-minute jog, every morning you may make a small adjustment to your routine by telling yourself, *Let me start small.*

1. Every time the phone rings, get up and walk while finishing the conversation.
2. After dinner, walk for 15 minutes.

These are simple things that can be done, without massive effort. Because what you need to remember, that the only way to rewire is to be your own coach.

Only you can help yourself take charge and put yourself back in control?

You are in charge of energizing your spirit, focusing your attention and keeping yourself impassioned.

Once you take the responsibility for yourself, you will never need anyone else to prod or push you into activating your own best efforts.

You are your own *internal life coach.*

You are your best friend, your closest ally, your strongest believer.

Only you can see the best in yourself and help yourself.

Give yourself the gift of purpose, guidance, direction, resolve and *unquestioned* belief and rewrite your self-concept.

You are loyal to you.
You are your ultimate motivator.
But how are you going to change the wiring and programming of your brain and get there?

Watch your words today and notice when you are being unkind to yourself or others. Gently remind yourself that you choose peace. Apologize to yourself and begin again.

5

Small Talk And a Lifetime Of Limitations

In order to minimize the negative experiences that are going to form imprints on your brain, you must develop an aversion to small talk, loose talk and conversations that have no sanctity or need about them.

Yes, you heard me right. I would recommend books like *Quiet: The Power of Introverts in a World That Can't Stop Talking*, to validate my statement.

Extended families, casual acquaintances and sometimes even immediate family, do much harm in this context; look at these statements:

1. Alcoholism runs in your family, doesn't it?
2. You will grow up to be plump like your aunt—you are both so similar!
3. Your classmate is actually smarter; just accept it.
4. Why do you always make silly mistakes in your papers?
5. You have no control over the amount of junk you eat.
6. Is there even one thing that you're really good at?
7. We don't have the money for this.
8. Your father tried many business ventures but failed

every time. What makes you think you'll succeed?
9. Why can't you be normal, like everyone else?
10. Do you really trust yourself to do this?
11. You're just going to cook and clean right?
12. Women should be dignified and not raise their voice.

The list is endless!

If these conversations are happening between distant relatives or acquaintances, then the fact is that you are not truly vested in the content and the giver/ recipient of the conversation. So you can easily learn to ignore everything that doesn't serve you.

Replace the negative suggestion with a new thought and spare yourself these experiences, every single time.

But what if it's your immediate family? Parent-child conversations for instance?

What about the parent who tells their child, 'You're just not serious enough about your work'?

Or 'You're an embarrassment to this family.'

Or husband-wife conversations? 'Because of you, I'm not able to grow in my career.'

Perhaps brother-sister conversations. 'How come you're so dumb that you don't get this simple concept?"

These conversations will matter to you and hence leave an imprint.

Often, some allegations are even worse:

'You never accept your mistakes.'

'Why can't you just admit that you messed up!'

Sometimes, the world places a major premium on honesty and throws you back into an abyss of self-loathing, a feeling that you are not good enough.

'Why don't you admit that you're not good enough?', comes

the suggestion.

This can be exhausting especially if you know that you need to move on.

A ten-minute argument with someone close to you first thing in the morning dumps so many toxic chemicals into your brain that it takes the whole day to get back to neutral.

You may have heard of this bizarre but true tale: In the Solomon Islands, if a tree needs to be cut down and it is too big to be chopped down, it is brought down by the combined efforts of the islanders cursing and yelling at the tree. This negative energy somehow damages the tree's life energy—after about thirty days of getting cursed the tree dies off and falls to the ground!

This is exactly what happens to you when you don't believe in yourself. If you are cursing yourself innumerable times a day, your self-esteem too will fall apart.

How can you re-programme your internal monologue? How do you respond when people confuse 'berating yourself' with honesty?

You are what your deep, driving desire is.
As your desire is, so is your will.
As your will is, so is your deed.
As your deed is, so is your destiny.

THE UPANISHADS

6

Reprogramme Your Internal Monologue

The earlier chapter has a rather scientific explanation of the workings of our brain. Here is a much simpler one.

Our brain operates very much like a personal computer. Even though an adult human brain weighs just about 1,400 gm and about 2 per cent of the total body weight, the brain is far more complex than the most powerful computers we have created.

Let's use the analogy of a computer. A computer has three parts:

1. A monitor—this is what you display.
2. A keyboard—this is our experiences, what we hear, see, taste, touch and smell.
3. A hard drive—this is your control centre, where all your wiring is, your subconscious.

For this generation that is intensely familiar with computers, understanding the parallels of how the mind works is easy. Please note that this is a very simplified way of putting the complex workings of the human mind.

Any computer can operate only on the basis of the programmes fed into it. If you install a new software into the hard drive of your computer, on your command, it will read instructions from the new programme and respond accordingly. You can delete the old programme to make space for a new one. What is stored within is what will come out. The brain operates in the same way.

From the day you were born, you have been fed numerous kinds of software. These are a result of the thoughts and experiences you have programmed into yourself. Or what others have programmed into you.

As dependents, children have no choice but to listen and believe what others say. Children can be quite powerless that way and cannot choose the environment they have to survive in.

There is a 'command centre' that develops within, that has an existing understanding of your capabilities—your beauty, nature and everything else that defines you. You are told what to expect, what to believe in, how to act and what to do or not to do.

Every time you have to respond to a situation, your brain reaches out for a response, via electrical impulses, to this command centre. This then affects, directs and controls everything about you. To change the way you respond, you have to change the software which is fed within.

In order to make a difference to the way you treat yourself or speak to yourself, you have to work at two levels simultaneously—the external and the internal.

The external level is based on the philosophy that your brain is designed to change and is open to being re-programmed throughout your lifetime. So you focus on the following:

1. Observing your thoughts: Listen to everything you say to someone else, everything you say when you talk to yourself, or about yourself. Additionally, for the next two days, even listen to the thoughts you're thinking. Listen when you're exercising, walking or just doing something around the house. Observe whether your interactions and mental monologues elevate you or run you down.
2. Start deleting all the bad messages: Every time you choose a thought or are in an environment that doesn't serve you or make you feel good about yourself, press the edit button. Don't say them, don't think them, don't use them at all in your conversations. You deserve better.
3. Rewire your brain with repetition of an affirmative thought. Editing will stop the weeds from growing, but won't plant the flowers. Choose a new thought that serves you. Say it, use it, share it and experience it.

The problem with focusing on external rewiring alone is the question of how to sustain it.

Although you may spend your life killing, you will not exhaust all your foes. But if you quell your own anger, your real enemy will be slain.

—NAGARJUNA

7

Why Do We Put Off Self-improvement For Another Day?

Most of us know we can do much better. Deep in our hearts, we know we could have started our day by planning it, or got up earlier in the morning and gone for a jog.

In fact, even when we are eating a lazy breakfast on a Sunday morning, we feel guilty about skipping the morning exercise and make a mental plan to play cricket at 4 p.m.

And then at 4 p.m., in the middle of an afternoon siesta, we press the snooze button. It's tea time thereafter, and a plan is made to watch a movie and have dinner outside.

As we amble back home at 11 p.m. there is no energy left for a workout. And it's Monday the next morning—so goodnight!

I'll begin to exercise from next week, you tell yourself. You also tell yourself that you have merely put it away for 'now', not cancelled the plan—you will eventually do better.

Just not today.

This is the story of many of us. Many of us would readily agree that we too, would like to improve *something* about ourselves, however small.

We are also aware of the benefits which creating small, incremental, improvements in ourselves creates in our lives. We crave many things:

1. More 'me time',
2. More freedom to do things we love, such as pursue hobbies.

Self-improvement is a bitter tablet. The discipline of having this foul-tasting pill, day after day, takes lots of grit and perseverance.

I applaud those who have made the transformation happen, to the other side where achievement and happiness become effortless parts of their lives.

But if you're one of those who could not despite wanting to change, if you didn't find a way to self-improvement that works for you, then keep reading.

Human history has proved that the normal distractions of everyday living are enough to keep even the most sincere individual from allocating the time or the energy to persevere and get ahead.

One other problem you have to prepare yourself to face is that you will often make things difficult for yourself along the way.

You have to keep things simple.

All of us have at some point seen advertisements on TVC Skyshop for the slim-shaper or tummy-cruncher or home fat-burner or home appliances like the french fry cutter or all-in-one juicer or yoga mats and DIY kits.

The advertising is persuasive. Men and women seem to work out effortlessly on tv, to get toned abs. Then comes a chef who makes perfect looking french fries in a jiffy with the cutter.

You know what!

There's nothing fundamentally wrong with any of those products in terms of perceived utility or functionality.

Let's start with the exercise machines; no matter how good they are, they won't work if you don't use them regularly. Most of these machines need assembling, setting up, putting away after use and some even take up space in the bedroom.

And even with the sincerest among us, anything that takes too much time, requires too much sacrifice, or is too complex to use easily, will not get used.

The home exercise machines, which require assembly, get put away. Even while putting them away, you tell yourself that it's only a temporary situation. You will bring them out soon.

And then, one day, when you're cleaning the house, about ten different machines and appliances, too cumbersome to use (in hindsight) get thrown or given away.

I can give you other examples of things that we postpone:

1. Replacing TV remote batteries: You can keep tapping, removing the batteries and switching their places, and sometimes it works too! But buying new batteries won't happen unless it actually threatens your TV viewing completely.
2. Repairing a drawer at home that doesn't close fully: You keep kicking it every day but calling the carpenter is something you put off, till it becomes a fight at home.
3. Exercising (!)
4. Making a phone call to your mom and dad, asking them how they are, or making a plan to take them out for a movie.
5. Getting up early.

Self-improvement is not just about self-talk but also about rethinking your routines, so you have to pay attention to the small things.

> *A man must first despise himself, and*
> *then others will despise him.*
>
> MENCIUS

8

Unshackling the Chains Of Habit

The external rewiring discussed earlier only works for some time and then the average individual will revert to his old ways.

After the first excitement of the brand new 'listening-editing-repeating' wears off, the dreams soon give way to the realities of everyday living.

Evolution dictates that old programming controls our habits, and hence, they will take over once again.

The new understanding of conquering the world and making great changes is 'postponed'. When you make a resolution to stay healthy, you make a healthy diet chart, full of fruits, sprouts and salads and follow it religiously for a week. Then it's back to the old way, just like before, living life as we always have, maybe getting a little ahead or getting by, and then falling back into your comfort zone. Suddenly, you wonder why you aren't doing as well as you think you should.

New ideas—for learning a new online course, making more money, being better managers, getting organized, losing weight—which have you hooked for exactly three months or less, fall by the wayside.

Self-help books that rule many cocktail dinners and parties

become once-read books sitting forgotten on shelves.

Every successful behavioural researcher or spiritual guru has always spoken of 'visualizing' and holding close to your mind, the picture of you that you most want to live. Whatever you put into your mind—in *one way or another*—is what you will get back out—in *one way or another.*

But how do you make it 'stick' and 'stay' and not relapse into the old ways.

If you want to be deeply committed to self-transformation, you have to focus on your internal rewiring.

Imagine that you're a painter and you need to gather your easel, canvas, paints, brushes and whatever other tools you need. You have done a lot of work on what you intend to paint. All this is your prep before you even start painting.

Similarly, there's a prep to your commitment to transformation. Feeding your mind a foundation based on good philosophy is the foundation where you need to start.

There are great philosophers all over the world—Plato, Socrates, Aristotle, Jalaluddin Rumi, Confucius, Emmanuel Kant, Avicenna, Mencius, Gautama Buddha, Lao Tzu—so pick up any work that you believe will to enrich your mind.

And whether you're a young man or woman in Shanghai, Peru, New York, Dubai, Johannesburg, Sydney, Delhi or Rio, any philosophy in the world that gives you roots will ground you to a basic foundation, one on which you can build a whole new approach to yourself.

I have been deeply influenced by thinkers such as Sir Aurobindo, Bodhidharma, Kabir, Swami Vivekananda, Ramakrishna Paramhansa, Nagarjuna. And I will be quoting them often to share the powerful wisdom they have bequeathed us. Not because I'm the expert on it, but because I have lived it. And it helped me emerge victorious from my travails. It is not too heavy, neither is it too voluminous and it is most certainly not intimidating.

To act without clear understanding, to form habits without investigation, to follow a path all one's life without knowing where it really leads; such is the behaviour of the multitude.

MENCIUS

9

The Spiritual Way To Tame the Monster In Your Head

It is possible to tame the monster in your head. Arm yourself with focus and determination. You can do this, if you commit to it.

You can read the five steps, which have been given here. But to truly understand each step, you have to turn to the relevant chapter that discusses each step in detail.

1. Connect to your source: Your soul craves a very different set of things. Your soul knows you have greatness within you, even though your mind may not. Your soul is stirred by the idea of you expanding and removing any and all limitations. This is another form of mindfulness itself—where you become more connected to the present moment and increase your full awareness of your internal and external experiences.

2. Opt out of being ordinary: You're expected to live a life that everyone can understand and accept at the level of ordinary consciousness, which generally means accepting whatever life gives you. In many

ways, you've been programmed to believe that *you do not* possess the wisdom or ability to manifest the complete scope of your potential and your wishes. Start actively challenging these non-serving thoughts and beliefs—especially the ones that seem so deeply ingrained in you that you may take them completely for granted. Even if you have spent a great deal of your life simply 'going through the motions', you can make the choice *right now* to begin to develop new beliefs.

3. Activate your imagination: As the Creator created you, so you create your future. And you are dependent on one thing above all—your own imagination. The greatest gift you were ever given was the gift of your imagination. Within your magical inner realm is the capacity to live the life of your dreams, the life that the full extent of your abilities should provide you with. Your imagination is your domain for creating the life that you desire, and the best part of it is that you are the monarch of this kingdom! You have the inherent powers to rule your world as you desire.

4. Master your emotions: Learn how to consciously connect with your body. Practise tuning into how your body is feeling, noticing areas of tension or stress. Increase your overall conscious experience through becoming more aware of your bodily reactions to thoughts, feelings and events. Acknowledge your biases and limited perspectives. Continually challenge your knowledge and assumptions. If you encounter something new, choose to learn more about it rather than brush it off. Expand your intellectual horizons.

5. Find your values: Having a clear sense of what matters most to you enables you to take up a small fight that matters to you and therefore overcome apathy and indifference. Values act as guideposts that direct your behaviour and shape your goals in useful ways. Make the choice to become an active or lifelong learner.

The knowledge of anything, since all things have causes, is not acquired or complete, unless it is known by its causes.

—AVICENNA

RESCRIPTING YOUR LIFE—THE HOW

*If you refuse to assume the responsibility
to find a higher self inside yourself, then you are
your worst enemy.*

10

Stage 1: Connect To Your Source

You are not a drop in the ocean.
You are the entire ocean in a drop.

—JALALUDDIN RUMI

1993: Wisdom at ₹20

If you've been to the city of Mumbai, you will know that the city streets have footpaths that sell books for as little as ₹20.

On my way to the British Council Library, one day, just after my twelfth standard had begun, I found a pocket-sized yellow book with the picture of Swami Vivekananda on it for ₹20. This was 1993.

The book had a sentence that read: 'Cause is never different from effect, the effect is but the cause reproduced in another form.'

My first thought was *Blah blah blah blah*!

But wait. Something made me read it again.

'Cause is never different from effect. The effect is but the cause reproduced in another form.'

So if I give you a gift (cause) and you love me back for it (effect), then a physical gift of love is reproduced into my life as love received from you.

Made perfect sense! The cause and the effect carry themselves within each other.

Another way to understand this is as follows:

The wave is the same thing as water; the effect is the cause in another form.

Got this!

We, we, and no one else, are responsible for what we suffer. We are the effects, and we are the causes.

I was hooked!

Without the first two sentences in the same book by Swami Vivekananda, the third one would not have made any sense on its own to me.

Being without any real friends at the time, I started devouring books about such philosophies at a very early age.

I read the gist of everything around that time—in whatever was available on the street and whatever I could afford—the pocket-friendly versions of the Upanishads and the torn, decrepit versions of the Gita. They all seemed to say just one thing—that the life I had is a miracle, and I am responsible for whatever I make of it.

So instead of blaming someone else for what I was going through, I had to take charge. And I had already wasted many years.

Many of these kind of booksellers had got used to me ambling around their stalls and browsing. I was oblivious to my surroundings and would go into a daze, perching uncomfortably, yet assuredly on any little grip or crevice that any wall offered.

I think it was quite evident to the booksellers that I was no millionaire, and wouldn't buy much, but having a customer hanging around makes other customers stop by too. So I had many hours of apolaustic, uninterrupted reading.

Look inwards. Take time to discover yourself. Appreciate something small about yourself, and acknowledge the purpose that you hold dear to your heart. Learn to love yourself, your thoughts, your values and your ideals. If you have never tried it, start now. Cherish it. Master your senses. Always speak and think well about yourself. You start reflecting this positivity, and people see you as a person radiating warmth.

Your source and your immensity

What is your source? The Creator, who created the entire universe, and is immense and omnipresent, is your source.

In order to fully understand the process that will lead you to 'freedom' from negativity and to connect with this powerful source, I must use a catalyst.

My catalyst is some of the incisive observations of the great Swami Vivekananda, the chief disciple of the nineteenth-century Indian mystic Ramakrishna Paramahamsa.

Swami Vivekananda was a key figure in the introduction of the Indian philosophies of yoga and the Vedanta all over the world. I have taken the liberty to simplify some of his sayings.

Read each sentence twice.

You are at Stage 1 of vanquishing the monsters of the negative mental monologues that have cultured your life up to this point, and if you do not cross this stage, you cannot progress to Stage 2.

Once you finish the book, come back and read the wisdom of Swami Vivekananda again.

1. Existence cannot be produced by non-existence. Something cannot come out of nothing. The law of causation is omnipotent and knows no time or place when it did not exist.
2. The seed comes out of the tree; it does not immediately become a tree, but has a period of inactivity or rather, a period of very fine un-manifested action. The seed has to work for some time beneath the soil. It breaks into pieces, degenerates as it were. Regeneration emerges out of the degeneration.

3. Since the universe exists, it must have come out of something because it was very easy to see that nothing comes out of nothing, anywhere. All work that is done by human hands requires material. If a house is built, the material was in existence before. If a boat is made, the material existed before. If any implements are made, the material existed before. Hence, the effect is produced. Naturally, therefore, the first idea that this world was created out of nothing was rejected, and some material out of which this world was created must have already been in existence!
4. If you mean to say there is a Being entirely separate from this universe, who has created you and this universe just by His will—out of nothing—that cannot be proved. Such a state of things cannot be.
5. Nobody has ever seen anything produced out of nothing; if anything arises in the mind, that also must have been produced from something. When we speak of free will, we mean that the will is not caused by anything. But that cannot be true, the will is caused; and since it is caused, it cannot be free.
6. Everything that I do or think or feel, every part of my conduct or behaviour, my every movement—all is caused and therefore not free.

Can you accept that what is within you is itself a part of the process of Creation?

You are made up of the same source as this immense, powerful universe, and have all the qualities of this powerful source!

The cause of you being here is your source

We have all been created from the same source. And there has to be a 'source', because as Swami Vivekananda said nothing can come from nothing.

So you must have some properties similar to the source that you came from.

In Sanskrit, there is a wonderful word called aadi, which is an interesting synthesis of the connotation of the words, source and beginning.

We will call this source our aadi.

Every religion in the world honours aadi in its own way—this source is free of the labels of caste, creed or religion.

We all came from this common aadi in one form. Over time, our form kept changing constantly (due to age) but retained all the elements of the creative energy that we came from.

There is a spark of the aadi within you that you cannot fathom. It is that which you cannot grasp with the senses—it causes your heart to beat, your hair to grow and your lungs to inhale and exhale. You've become accustomed to taking it for granted.

You now put your physical reality and desires ahead of this deep and colossal knowledge and power within you. You don't realize the real power vested within you until it is too late.

My objective is to inspire you to recognize that the source energy—a tiny fragment of aadi—is located within you, and to help you increase the power of that fragment so it becomes the primary force in your everyday life.

I'm encouraging you to conceptualize that tiny fragment of aadi that is located within you.

Imagine it growing to double its size and multiplying till

it becomes the real you, becoming visible through your loving and inviting attention, and all the good experiences you focus on. As you tell your mind to change the narrative, and feed it with thoughts and experiences of your own immensity, capacity and power, you will be able to feel this connection.

You will now feel the sacred presence of your higher self as the companion light of your life, the foundation of your life.

Now you have a big piece of aadi to assist you in attaining the fulfilment of your wishes—know that it was within you all along.

Put your higher self to work every day.

You are aadi and aadi is you

There is nothing that this higher self within you cannot accomplish.

Your awareness that God isn't something external to you but within you will confound you at first. This will change your dialogue with yourself completely.

This image that we have of God as a 'giver' is suddenly contradictory. How funny that God knows how to heal, but yet withholds healing from some and offers it to others who are presumed to have paid some kind of dues.

Many of us also live under the assumption that God plays favourites. This is ridiculous and harmful.

The human concept of God is as someone who doles out punishments, gets angry and demands sacrifices and rituals.

Really?

Living in the aadi level of awareness tells you that the energy of God is within you and then the fulfilment of your wishes becomes natural.

There is no one outside you who can grant and take away your wishes. Because you are the origin and you are the universe. And that's the software you feed into yourself.

No one gives joy or sorrow.
We gather the consequences of our own deeds.

—GARUDA PURANA

The illusion of separation that leads to depression

The Upanishads say, 'As is the atom, so is the universe.'

You and the universe are therefore a continuum. Not separate, but one.

The human challenge is to eliminate the illusion of separation. To live out of the knowledge that we are each of the same substance and we will return to the same source.

Let's make this simpler. If you ask person A and person B how they find the world, both will give different answers.

For person A, the world is beautiful and the people are good, while for person B, the world is extremely bad, and the people are treacherous and sinful.

The outer world is the projection of your inner world. Therefore, the only way to improve the world outside is to improve the world within.

Let us go back to the topic of depression, which is primarily the inability to accept the circumstances you are in.

Depression is therefore just a lack of spiritual experience of life. What you need is mindfulness. Then you can accept that the only victories to be gained are over your own self.

You will then have renewed strength to gain more victories over yourself.

Meet this transient world with neither grasping nor fear, trust the unfolding of life.

—BHAGAVAD GITA

11

Stage 2: Opt Out Of Being Ordinary (Embracing THECO)

Arise—transcend thyself. Thou art man and the whole nature of man is to become more than himself.

—SRI AUROBINDO

My story in brief

I am writing this in the spirit of disclosure.

If I haven't overcome exacting circumstances of my own, or had significant spiritual epiphanies over time, what is my qualification to preach?

1986: Monotony and self-talk

It was 3.30 p.m. I was ten years old. I placed one foot in front of the other, my legs moving forward, almost aimlessly it seemed. School was over and I had to go home—though I didn't want to.

My sister Renu would either reach before me or after me.

I crossed the shops I crossed every day—Chedda Stores (dhishkyaooon) and Manoj Stationery (skadooosh)!

I was firing imaginary bullets at names that had settled themselves in my memory. I even knew the faces of the people who would be manning those stores at that hour.

That old chashmish (bespectacled) uncle would be reading a Gujarati paper. At 3.30 in the afternoon? What on earth had he been doing all day? That's pretty late to know what's going on around the world.

I used to reach school early to read the library copy of the newspaper, in order to sound smart during the day.

I dreaded going home. Home was so boring. Maybe I could go to my teacher Indira Menon's house. She would offer me a Rasna or something!

My habits got the better of me and I reached home, unlocked the front door and got in.

I headed straight to the dabba of rotis. There would be four rotis—two for Renu, two for me. I gobbled them up gratefully, changed and started reading.

Renu came by shortly afterwards, and tuned the radio station to BBC—'The news, on the hour, every hour'—it said.

1987: Pangs of jealousy

I wasn't raised in any particular religious faith, probably because my parents were too busy commuting to office and back, and spending their weekends trying to catch up on sleep.

I used to look at them, and realize that they always did things that they had to, never what they wanted to. Except, perhaps, sleeping on weekends.

My mother used to pass jewellery shops and sari shops,

claiming she didn't want a thing, and my dad would buy her a samosa, knowing fully well that it didn't match up. But that was them—there were days when they were happy about nothing, and days when they were decidedly unhappy about everything.

I learnt to value choice very early in life. Because I assumed my parents' meagre life and the apparent drudgery of their existence were the sum total of their own choices.

But I held steadfast to the notion—I was God's chosen one. Probably because once an astrologer had said some pretty nice things about me. I consciously decided to let that 'better future' programme stay within me, and define my actions.

School was a protected environment, so all my notions were never challenged.

There were a few rich children in my school. Sandhya Menon's dad dropped her to school in a big white Ambassador car every morning. Amol Pednekar's tiffins used to be delicious—garlic bread, pasta, parathas, sweets, the works. His tiffin had five compartments!

And you should have seen Meghana Ruparel's pencil boxes—very cutting-edge and a new one every month. And Vinayak's home, a massive bungalow, was right next to school.

Most kids also bought new uniforms every year. I had to do two years in one uniform, and this one was going above the knee. So Amma brought some matching fabric and extended the length. It looked weird but I decided not to care about it.

I was told 'if you study hard, you'll get a good job'. I assumed good job meant money. So I grew up knowing that I had to put my head down and make the right choices—in order to be able to make better choices tomorrow.

And the right choice in childhood meant that I would

study the hell out of every goddamned book that I laid my hands on.

The biggest question I wanted answered as a child was, why wasn't my father like everyone else's? You know, like those guys who look 'dependable'?

1988: Appa

I would get three new dresses every year—on Diwali, my birthday and the school annual day. The bonus gifts would be from my uncle's trips from Dubai or Muscat.

One that day, walking back home, I was wondering why Kannan Uncle had not visited us in a long time. The shampoo, thick Nivea cream and chocolates were eluding me.

As I reached out for my key to my bare apartment surrounded by slums, I noticed it was unlocked.

I rang the doorbell.

A red face, seriously troubled by mental imbalance, opened the door.

It was Appa.

I avoided his gaze as I entered home. His face was red. I knew what that meant.

I opened the roti dabba quietly. It was empty. Appa must have eaten the rotis. Appa was having a cup of coffee. He had his suitcase on his lap and was writing something. Next to him, a tape recorder was playing. He had written a Telugu song for a super hit movie and got paid ₹5,000 for it.

He was happy—as he told me.

He didn't greet me. I didn't know whether to care. I also didn't ask if he had eaten my evening rotis. I could see the plate—he must have been hungrier than I was. He had got some laddoos and gave me one. I was grateful and had it quietly.

I didn't hate him. I just hated what he seemed to be doing to Amma. And I had all sorts of questions about him in my head.

'Are you studying hard to become an IAS officer?' came Appa's voice.

'Yes,' I said.

I wondered whether I should show him my report cards, but his red face and three lines drawn over his forehead with sandalwood were a little too scary.

I knew he was on a 'high'.

Between Renu and I, the meaning was very simple: when Appa was high, he was impossible. His face would be red, he would tie a belt over his lungi and wear a flashy shirt. He had no bad habits. High was a mental state of hyper-excitement that he couldn't control.

He must have got some movie assignment, someone must've promised him big money and that must have got him 'high'. He would shout if he was asked anything and he would leave the house again in a few days, saying that the world was ready to welcome a new superstar, or some such proclamation.

I was too young to understand the whole relationship thing between a man and a woman, a husband and a wife. But I knew this—Amma was terribly lonely and very uncared for.

For instance, look at Sandhya Menon's mom. She did nothing all day except twiddle her thumbs. But when she stepped out, she had skin that was always glowing, with well-done hair and crisp-ironed saris. She was a housewife but walked around like a diva.

My mother—very hardworking and making just enough

money to pay all the bills—wore unironed blouses with saris that were easy to wash and looked cheap. That defined her wherever she went.

Was it a fair world?

1989: Evening snacks

At 6.30 p.m. sharp, the doorbell rang.

It was Amma! The only person in the world who ever had good news or good food. Other than Principal Sahu Ma'am, who would often give me biscuits whenever I went to her room.

Today, Amma had two sponge cakes in her bag.

As Renu made coffee for Mom, I finished my sponge cake. Renu anyway helped around the house far more than I ever did. Renu, being four years older to me, must have seen much more of Appa's deviant behaviour. I wonder how it affected her. The other thing about her was that she was always more capable of forgiveness that I was.

There were two single beds in the hall, each of which had a study desk attached. Weird design, but that was all the space we had—495 square feet to call our home. I sat on mine and started doing my homework.

In-between answers, I asked in a very self-absorbed way, 'Amma, when are you going to get veg puffs for snacks?'

Mom's office had a snack system—every evening at 4, they would give some snack along with coffee. Mom's boss knew that we were not very well off, so he would give her his snack packet too.

Sponge cakes, veg puffs, samosas, a packet of potato chips, etc., were the usual snacks. Mom used to get two packets every evening for us. In the twenty years that she worked at

Hoechst Pharma, Mom never ate her evening snack.

1990: My THECO and how it became impregnable

THECO is my acronym for The Chosen One and a very major part of this mental monologue that is going on within all of us.

1990 was the year I realized that there was a THECO within me, which was unquestionable and unconquerable.

It was 1990. I was all grown up now, fourteen years old, and I thought I looked reasonably okay. A roadside Romeo had started timing my walks and stalking me on my way back from school. I had mentioned it to Mom once or twice, but she said what all Indian mothers say—'Don't look at him'; 'Don't give him any importance'; 'Come by some other way'.

I had only vaguely heard of words like rape. But I had no idea how mortifying it could be. And my building didn't have any watchman who would ask visitors their names or purpose for coming to the building.

After stalking me for a good month, this scoundrel figured out that I opened the lock every evening and was alone at home post school. And the only person who would come home after me was my sister.

It was a sultry Wednesday and I had a very bad feeling in my stomach. I was exhausted when I reached home. As I climbed the last flight of stairs and removed my keys to unlock the door, I could hear footsteps behind me. I didn't think much of it.

Out of curiosity, I turned back. To my shock, I saw this very reprobate roadside Romeo. With both my neighbours' doors locked, he had already planned this day.

I was trying to be quick on my feet, but I just didn't

know what to do. Should I take a chance and run up to the second floor and try my luck? Jincy's mom was a housewife and would be home.

And then the most unbelievable thing happened. The door to my house opened. From inside.

Mom was home early and I could hear her brother's voice from inside. This never happened even once before! But she was at home and Kannan Uncle, as we called him, was home too!

Someone was watching over me. I was the chosen one (THECO)! I had just been saved from God knows what!

The scoundrel, after hearing a man's voice from my house, beat a hasty retreat. I told my mom. We had a moment of silence. She looked helplessly back at me.

At that moment, knowing the number of battles she was fighting, I decided to reimagine my future and make her proud.

My THECO had laid its roots that day.

I never saw that rogue again! And I have no idea why he didn't try to come after me again.

1991: College

I was to finish the tenth standard and go to college. I was as old as a child could be before being called a young adult.

I had grown up watching my parents fight. Here's a standard conversation.

Appa: 'I am in this position because you never believed in me!'

Amma: 'What is there to all this belief nonsense? A cheque hits my bank account on the fifth of every month. Where's your cheque?'

Appa: 'Cheque, cheque, cheque! That's all you want! What about my dreams as a man? I could have achieved so much more if you had given me time!'

Amma: 'Time? Is that what you want? I married you when I was twenty. I am forty today. My elder daughter is nineteen and my younger daughter is fifteen. How much more time do you want before you start contributing to this family?'

Appa: 'Maybe I could've been a big filmmaker today if not for your big mouth which always speaks of doom.'

Amma: 'Where were you when school fees had to be paid and groceries had to be ordered? What have you been doing away from home twenty days a month? Pursuing your dreams? Or your madness?'

So on and so forth till it became two people slinging mud at each other—so much so that both got dirty.

Even though he was a nice man, somehow in-between his well-meaning intentions and his inability to fulfil his dreams, Appa had lost himself. Amma was too busy paying the bills to provide him emotional support.

The only sentence I remember Appa saying to me was 'You should become an IAS officer.'

Sometimes I would blame my mom for what happened to my dad. Did she ever support him at all? Emotionally? Reassure him that some day, if he kept at it, his dreams would come true too?

There were so many fairy tales about people who had persevered for decades and then gotten unexpected, unparalleled success. Was Appa one of those cases?

We will never know because Amma had made a choice—to pay the bills and give her kids an education.

Later in life, I realized I would be eternally grateful to her for the choices she made.

1988: Annual Day

I was miles ahead of the rest of my class.

The greatest days in school were report card days and annual days. I would carefully select mom's best sari and pester her to wear it. I had heard that this annual day—my sixth standard annual day—they were going to give away nice tiffins and water bottles to the best student.

My name was announced! Calling out Reeta Ramamurthy—English, first; Maths, first; Science, first; Geography, first; Hindi, first; History, first and overall rank, first in the entire class.

Yes! The bottle and the tiffin box were mine. And the tiffin box had four compartments.

There was one unwritten rule. After getting off the stage, I had to come straight to Amma.

Appa would also be sitting next to her, if he happened to be around. Because that was the high point of Amma's life.

All the big cars outside and big homes and fancy saris that the other moms wore didn't matter that day. I was her child, I was winning all the prizes and so by association, she was the 'super-achiever' mom.

Now for the T-ward science exhibition results. Best science exhibition project—Reeta Ramamurthy, standard six.

The prize looked big and I had forgotten about the science exhibition. What could it be?

It was a school bag and a free voucher for canvas shoes to wear to school! My current bag and shoes both had small holes.

I felt happy that I had earned all that I badly wanted by studying hard.

Now, for the inter-school elocution contest. The first prize for standard six was also me!

The last prize of the night was a brand new compass box!

This was one night when Sandhya Menon's Ambassador or the other girl Deeplakshmi's big bungalow just didn't matter.

The distance from the IIT convocation hall to home was a good 4 km, but we walked back slowly and grabbed some street food on the way so Amma wouldn't have to cook that night.

The light within me was lighting up my world—and Amma's world.

I think Appa's world too.

1989: My teenage vanities

It was my birthday.

One slice of cake, Eclairs to be distributed at school, one new dress and two new hairclips.

Mom would also buy one Big Bite at ₹35-burger that had just been launched. Samosas and chips would come home in the evening. And no roti/rice and vegetable if I didn't want to eat it.

Yay!

It was a thrilling day for me.

My new dress was a sky-blue-coloured frock, my most favourite one. I had seen pictures of Audrey Hepburn in the British Council Library, and as I scrubbed myself with soap and put talcum powder all over to smell fresh for the day, I thought I might look like her in that dress.

Today was important.

Stage 2: Opt Out Of Being Ordinary (Embracing THECO) • 55

I was going to be thirteen. I was a teenager. And I knew life was going to change. In some way—I have no idea how.

This day, 21 October 1989, was going to go down in history as the day when I found myself.

As I deluded myself with all these grandiose thoughts, Amma said that my uncle was coming from Muscat in the night!

I smiled. I knew exactly what that meant—vespertine enjoyment! A lavish dinner, plus a new shampoo, a new cream and at least one new foreign chocolate.

At school that day, I felt and behaved like Audrey Hepburn! What the heck—I was topping every subject any way and the morons in my batch weren't coming anywhere close to even scrubbing the floor I walked on. (Seriously vicious mind! Swag!)

But as I thought to myself, might as well enjoy a day of vanity.

The teachers were preoccupied with some official preparations and I was feeling quite free. The PT (physical education) teacher came to take two classes, and I got exempted because I was the birthday girl.

I detested the mud and dust of sport except for lawn tennis and Steffi Graf's game. Oh, how I loved her!

Here are two lines from a poem I had composed:

Her racket goes whip-wham
As she completed the Grand Slam

Stop clapping guys!

I even got a cheque of ₹30 from *The Indian Express*, which published my poem in one of its editions.

When I had received the cheque, Appa had told me that

I had his 'literary genes'. Another one of those sentences I didn't know how to react to.

As I prepared to leave school that day, it was the twin exasperating and opulent duo of Sandhya Menon and Priya Prakash getting into their Ambassadors that spoilt the day for me!

I wanted those wealth-infested hooters out of my face—now! Spoiling my special day for nothing.

Suddenly, completely out of character, Sandhya stopped the car, rolled down the window and asked me, 'Hey, shall I drop you home?'

It would certainly have been a nice ride, but she couldn't possibly see the horrendous surroundings of the structure that was my home! I'd never be able to face her again!

So I told her, 'No, I need to pick up a few things on the way.'

I smiled lamely, wanting to just sit and experience that air-conditioned monstrosity on four wheels.

'Oh!' she said, then added, 'Here's an invitation to my birthday party. Please come tomorrow.'

She held out a card that surely cost at least ₹10. I wondered how many she had bought. That was serious money being spent on a birthday invitation card! Which means there was more money being spent on the actual party.

This was even more bothersome. In school, I was the topper and I was the best. At annual days, all parents wanted to say hello to my mom. I ruled!

But a birthday party was like being in a ring where I wasn't the champion! I wasn't the ruler—she and her bothersome pestilential moneyed friends would rule and make fun of me. Besides, this blue dress was the only one I had. I would have to wash it and iron it again by tomorrow. Unless by some twist of fate, my uncle got me something tonight!

I walked home slowly, praying for a miracle.

The card said: 59, Radhakrishnan Street. What kind of an address was that? Just one number? No building name or flat number?

Hmmph!

One day, my address will be 10 Downing Street. Take that Sandhya Menon!

1991-93: The worst formative years

After school, I got admission into SIES College in Sion, Mumbai. While schooling was sheltered, college was a curious experience.

There were really pretty girls who captured everyone's attention. There were groups of people who had been friends in school and already knew each other. There were people there who were admitted through the management quota, who were far richer than anything I had seen in school.

I had all of four dresses and knew no one!

And worse, I just didn't like Physics. I was unbeatable at English and Maths—as always—and Professor Nerurkar, who used to teach us Maths, used to call me the IIT girl.

My eleventh and twelfth standards were horrible. In a new environment, where I still had to prove myself, I had never had a good answer to the question, 'What does your father do?'

A harmless simple question that friends asked each other, but for me it was the death knell. Other than a brief productive spell at NITIE during my fourth to sixth standards (easily the best years of our life), my father hadn't actually done much.

The last seven years had been living hell at home because he was always home. A job used to last six months, his mental imbalance would return and he would lose his job again.

I shrank inwards more than ever before. Because I was finally old enough to understand that I had to figure out more things in life than my peers.

I wanted to make friends, but friendship requires that you're willing to be open about your own life.

Appa's highs were getting worse and he had started bringing some really strange people home at odd hours when Amma wouldn't be around. They all claimed to be in the 'south film industry'. My teenage girl instinct told me they were crooks. But Appa, in his desperation and naiveté couldn't see it.

Back to college. The thing with friendship is that it requires openness. Friends come home, you go to their homes. But I wasn't in that space. I couldn't invite anyone home. And to top it all, I couldn't sleep at night.

Amma took me to a shrink. I was on sleeping pills for almost six months during that phase. I used the same prescription at different medical stores each time by getting rid of the date. By the end of my eleventh standard, I was a wreck.

This was the worst adjustment period of my life. I was hoping for a miracle.

Wandering aimlessly one day, just after my twelfth standard commenced, I found a 20-rupee pocket-sized yellow book with the picture of Swami Vivekananda on it at one of the book vendors on the street, on my way to the British Council Library. This was just after my eleventh standard.

That book said, 'Cause is never different from effect, the effect is but the cause reproduced in another form.'

I have taken you through my realizations here earlier in the book.

All kinds of books that I had never noticed before started coming forward into my field of vision, almost as if by design. Picking up books from the British Council Library, and reading on railway stations, was initially just a ploy to reach home as late as possible—preferably after Amma came home.

Being without many friends at the time, I read the gist of everything around that time—whatever was available on the street and whatever I could afford—translations of the Upanishads, the Gita. So while most of my peers were bracketing their lives into PCM (Physics-Chemistry-Maths) scores for engineering and PCB (Physics-Chemistry-Biology) scores for medicine, I was in a unique love affair with Indian philosophers.

Just look at this gem:

> 'The gold put in furnace loses its impurities and regains its original true nature. In the same way, through meditation, the mind gets rid of the impurities like delusion and attachment and attains the Reality, which is its true eternal state.'
>
> —Adi Shankaracharya

They all seemed to say just one thing—that despite the furnace my life seemed to have been put in, my life itself was a miracle, and I was responsible for whatever was in it. So, instead of blaming Appa for what I was going through, I had to take charge. Work with my THECO (The Chosen One) and reinforce good messages into my head.

That sounded tough! Really tough.

One day, while coming back from college, I overheard

a conversation in the local train. One well-dressed girl was telling another, 'My father is in real estate'. Hmm! What on earth did that mean?

But the listener was impressed.

Voila! It works!

I decided to stick with this answer and eliminate the cause—the question, what does your father do—by coming up with an effect—a prepared ambiguous answer.

But what choice did *I* have?

1993-96: A whole new world

I had changed overnight—if one year could be called that.

Yes, I had invented a lie, but it gave me some breathing space.

My twelfth-standard results were awful, and those who knew me, even marginally, were also shocked at the 83 per cent I got.

Amma was upset because she had been sure I would make it to a top engineering college like VJTI, an IIT or something similar.

But my mind wasn't there. I wanted to explore what I wanted to do for a few more years. I was beginning to understand that I had a powerful mind now—one that could overcome my present circumstances. And engineering wasn't my goal. Life was.

And since I stopped taking sleeping pills and started focusing on studying again, Amma relaxed a little bit.

Renu, four years older to me, had also doubtless been affected by our fragile, barely secure, turbulent childhoods. She proceeded to graduate and get a job in direct sales, which was a great training ground. We always loved each other but it wasn't something that needed to be uttered; it was understood—we had, after all, seen so much together.

I proceeded to consciously distance my mind from my circumstances. Even though, we were expected to live a 'normal' life that everyone could understand and accept, and mouth platitudes like 'But, what can I do?' or 'How can I help it if my father isn't a stable man?' I had decided to focus on change. And what I could do.

I was the chosen one, and I was going to live from my THECO awareness.

Maybe a fatalistic mindset had affected Renu a little more than me because she spent more time with Appa, and sympathized with him much more. The problem with sympathy is that soon, you begin to identify with the person.

But I refused to sympathize with Appa—it would make me weak in my support of Renu and Amma.

I wanted to stay as far away from that mindset as possible. There were three reasons for this:

1. I vaguely had an idea that Appa had a mental condition that needed treatment. We weren't really sure of it at the time. In the 1980s and 90s, psychological treatments were not as common as they are now. Amma was too busy being the breadwinner to think about mental ailments and their treatment.
2. The idea that her husband was mentally unstable was something she was living with. She had become so tight within herself that she lived her life local train to local train, morning to morning, without letting anything distract her.
3. She had given up and had indicated to Appa that she had given up on him too.

1995: Making a friend

It was a new, aware, detached mindset that allowed me to make my first real friend: Preeti Shetty.

I told her upfront that my father had a mental problem, and in acknowledging my deepest problem, in that moment, I had become free.

There were some firsts I have to credit Preeti with:

1. The first time I spent money to go out to a hotel for a meal—it was a lassi at GK, outside SIES College, Sion, for ₹12.
2. The first time I went for a movie—there were seven-eight of us. I think it was *Karan Arjun,* the Shah Rukh Khan–Salman Khan starrer.

Preeti had a very straightforward approach to life, and spoke her mind. I had not yet developed a mind that spoke anything out loud—I only spoke plenty inside my head.

So she was a revelation and I liked being with her.

I continued my graduation in SIES, an institution I was now familiar with.

As far as college was concerned, my behaviour was influenced by middle class south Indian family precepts: 'Good girls don't go to the college canteen.' 'Good girls don't get roses on rose day.' 'Good girls don't talk to boys about anything other than studies.'

My best friends continued to be books.

But I saw a whole new world during my graduation years. I had taken the first, tentative step towards accepting who I was. This acceptance was priceless. And I became comfortable with my circumstances.

1996: Breaking away

I had some dreams, first of becoming a pilot (couldn't afford that) and then to major in English literature.

Amma sat me down and told me to do an MBA.

'That's the only way you will get a high-paying job,' she said.

I got through Tata Institute of Social Sciences (TISS) and Symbiosis. I chose Symbiosis because it was my only chance to go away from home. As Amma cried a million buckets while leaving me behind in a paying guest accommodation in Pune, I didn't know what to do except to reassure her that I would get the best job that came to campus.

Over two years in Pune, I met sincere classmates, badass classmates, casual classmates, sutta-chai-ghazal-combo classmates, disco-dancing classmates, life-is-a-race-and-you-have-to-stay-ahead classmates, night owls, spoilt brats—the entire spectrum of students you could possibly meet.

Beyond their obviously rebellious behaviour, I must add that I met several remarkable people who are now living their dreams all over the world. I also met my future life partner.

But beyond all this, I knew that I had left Renu and my mom alone to fight an emotional war. But I rightly figured that I could help better if I made something of myself.

Something I had read in the Rig Veda stayed with me:

'The sacred flame of your inner shrine is constantly bright.'

So I focused on actualizing the best of what was within me. Day after day, I sent Renu and Amma my love and spoke to them in a million silent ways (that's Rumi again).

I had no idea how Mom coughed up my tuition fee. Knowing fully well that Amma would not have spare cash to even buy a sari in the two years that I was pursuing my MBA.

I dived into my studies with the vengeance of an Olympic swimmer.

1997: Reliving Kapil Dev

One day, in 1997, in the middle of my MBA, Renu got married. Mom put up a brave show, and thankfully Appa was there too.

My simple, beautiful sister was a shy bride. But it was all a blur for me. I would have liked to ask her so many questions—is the guy right for you? Are you escaping too?

But I figured that there are days when you do what family does. Just stick around.

Mom's office bosses would come, which meant that an AC hall had to be hired in Chembur, where all good south Indian marriages happen.

The four of us smiled together and stood together. Perhaps the last time we had all smiled together was the aloo wafer, samosa and chai night during the 1983 cricket world cup when Kapil Dev made us forget our worries for a day and the underdogs won.

Cricket, for most lower-middle class Indian families of the 80s, was an escape.

And Kapil Dev was a childhood hero, linked to the happiest childhood memory I have.

I decided to be thrilled that Renu had moved on. Happiness, after all, is a decision.

1998: My MBA graduation

It was 18 April 1998. Amma called. Appa had lost his last job too. He had met another film producer and wanted to write some new script for a telefilm. His unpredictable behaviour had started again.

She wanted to warn me because I was going to return home soon. The last time I was home, Appa had tried to hit me with bathroom slippers. This had been one of his worst episodes and Amma had hurt herself trying to stop him.

This was still fresh in my head. I hmm-ed through the call, as Amma wished me well, and told me that I had to ensure I got my degree and certificate and came back home safely to take up my campus placement in Reliance Industries.

She also reluctantly asked me if I wanted her to come for the graduation; the travel and hotel cost itself would be about ₹1,000.

I told her that it was perfectly okay if she didn't. After all, I was coming back to her. It was an uncomfortable conversation, but I had gotten used to it by now.

For the first time during the years of my education, Amma was not in the auditorium cheering.

1999: Appa moves on too

During the two years of my MBA, I had gotten used to being free of the constant shadow of failure and despair that had ruled my childhood because of Appa's unpredictable life.

After I began my job at Reliance Industries, in their Telecom division, like all silly youngsters, I bought a car within the first three months.

Within six months, I found stability. I got used to the money I was earning and started thinking more sensibly. I took over more responsibility.

Then there was the fact that I would one day settle down with the man I was seeing. So I spoke to Mom about moving from Mumbai to Chennai with me.

If she could relocate to Chennai, she would also have more family support. Her mom and siblings were all in Chennai. But it was not an easy decision.

First, I had to quit a happy, well-paying job and find a new job in Chennai. I was happy to do it.

Then Amma had to get a transfer.

And there was Appa, who had, once again disappeared. Seeing no recourse, Amma reluctantly agreed.

We bought a house, moved to Chennai and decided to be happy. Amma waited for Appa to join us. There was no sign of him.

Suddenly, in July 1999, we received news that Appa died in a train accident.

This was yet another situation in life where I didn't know how to react. Renu was absolutely inconsolable. I was neither sad, nor happy; I was only thinking about Amma.

Because after all the crazy days she had endured, if there was one thing she would have had in her old age, it was Appa's company.

This was taken away from her, and for the first time in her life, after a courageous innings in which she raised two daughters, ignored all her desires and faced all kinds of challenges, Amma looked defeated.

I wondered, why now—when we were so close to coming out of it—when Appa's role wasn't going to be that of a breadwinner, but a friend to Amma.

Maybe I could've got him that medical treatment too. I could afford it now.

I was desolate. Amma was heartbroken.

As a few days passed, Amma joined work again. She refused to let go of her colourful saris and bindi—and refused to pander to the custom for widows to wear white.

Renu and I never bothered; we believed that she should do whatever small thing could make her happy.

Most humbly we bow to You, O Supreme Lord.
At Your command moves the mighty wheel of time.
You are eternal, and beyond eternity.

—ARTHARVA VEDA

Understanding THECO

Enough about my story for now.

The real secret—of me being able to opt out of being ordinary—is that I believed I was The Chosen One. Since that day in '93, when my potential rapist walked away from my door, never to be seen again.

Having the THECO belief on my side helped shaped my life. It helped me focus and work. I always imagined myself as the saviour of my family, guided by the Supreme Power.

You too have a THECO attitude within you, residing in your aadi. Let's work on giving a voice to it.

I'm inviting you to be receptive to a new idea about yourself, an idea removed from the manic monstrosity of your negative mental monologue. It's radical because ever since you were born, you've been expected to be 'normal'.

You're expected to live a life that everyone can understand and accept at the level of ordinary consciousness, which generally means accepting whatever life has given you.

In many ways, you've been programmed to believe that you do not possess the wisdom or the ability to be able to experience the complete scope of your wishes and desires. You have decided to 'settle' at a certain level because you think this is how life is supposed to be, and that you're ordinary.

Let's call this the AIGE level—this is where you ask yourself, *Am I good enough*?

Can you opt out of this AIGE level?

Amma lived at the AIGE level for most of her life. She dealt with her unhappy marriage as God's will, and endured it. She never even thought that there could be an alternative life that she could build for herself.

So what's wrong with doing all of the things that your culture and your family programmed you to do?

There is absolutely nothing wrong with enduring your life—if it makes you happy. If that is the case, you can keep this book down and go about your life.

But, if you've decided to read on, then you believe you're capable of more.

As Amma lived her life, resigned to her fate, somewhere along the way, she willingly suspended many of her dreams, economic or otherwise, by thinking they were out of her reach.

She kept telling herself that she wasn't worth more. Perhaps she didn't have anyone to tell her otherwise.

Hear me loud and clear—the only way to bring all your dreams within your reach is to be willing to change your concept of yourself from AIGE to something else.

To THECO.

The value of acronyms like AIGE and THECO

I have realized that acronyms aid recall, and that is why I'm using them.

Within you is the capacity for imagination, connecting the dots, expansion and immensity. The one thing it needs more than anything else is to be free to expand, reach out and embrace miracles.

This happens only at the THECO level. THECO simply is your belief that you're the universe's chosen one. You and the universe are one and the same, even though you may not see it.

Here's a story from the Upanishads, a conversation between a father and his son.

The father said, 'Place this salt in water and bring it here tomorrow morning.'

The boy did as he was asked.

'Where is that salt?' his father asked, adding, 'I do not see it. Sip this and tell me how it tastes.'

The boy said, 'Salty, father.'

'And here? And there?' his father asked again.

'I taste salt everywhere,' he replied.

'It is everywhere, though we see it not. Just so, dear one, the self is everywhere, within all things, although we see it not. There is nothing that does not come from it. It is the truth; it is the self supreme. You are that, Shvetaketu. You Are That.'

The greatest secrets of the universe are within you, even though you may not be able to see them. This THECO-level consciousness resides in the depths of your soul.

Your soul craves a very different set of things. Your soul knows you have greatness within you, even though your mind may not be aware of it. You have to tell your brain about your vast potential via the wiring of your internal monologue.

Your soul is stirred by the idea of you expanding and removing any and all limitations.

Your new concept of the self is one inspired by your soul. This is the THECO level, where you believe that it is your light that lights up the world.

In the words of a scholar and famous seeker of truth, Adi Shankaracharya—whose eloquence, wisdom and a deep understanding on the ancient Indian scriptures are awe-inspiring—'To escape oneself from bondage, a wise person must exercise the right discrimination between True-self and the Ego-self. Only this discrimination can fill you with joy.'

THECO is not so much a level as it is a realization, an attitude and a way of life.

You truly believe that the universe is offering you its best; and live with that belief. Always. Even on the worst days.

The force of your 'natural wiring' rules the transition from AIGE to THECO.

What is your AIGE (Am I Good Enough) level?

It is that part of you that constantly worries whether you're going to get everything you want.

At the AIGE level, the predominant software programmes inside you are worry and low self-esteem.

AIGE includes your outer concept of yourself—everything you believe about your inborn as well as acquired talents and abilities.

You define yourself as prone to allergies or likely to gain weight, inclined toward skin rashes, or that you love sleep, or that

Stage 2: Opt Out Of Being Ordinary (Embracing THECO) • 71

you cannot sleep till 2 a.m. Statements such as 'I'm good with numbers', 'I'm good with words', beliefs about your intelligence, skills, musical and artistic talents and behavioural traits such being shy or confident, etc., comprise your outer AIGE level.

Your outer AIGE level contains a range of self-descriptors regarding this thing that you call your physical person. You grow up regarding them as the absolute truth.

Your inner AIGE level comprises how your mental monologues have shaped your belief systems, your values, what you tell yourself every day about your priorities, the working of your mind, your religious and spiritual beliefs and your points of view about how far your beliefs can carry you, whether your mind is capable of the intense rigour required to make the shift from your harmful, unspoken inner dialogues to favourable ones. The gumption and energy you grant to yourself.

You must know that your outer and inner AIGE levels are essentially a set of excuses to wriggle out of everything that you don't want to do.

But is it true that you can become anything that you want? After you make the transition from AIGE to THECO?

Can you become anything that you focus your attention to? Or is this some idealistic mumble jumbo?

I promised you one thing right at the beginning—this is a 'practical' self-help book. We will focus on what works!

So here's the first thing you must know, which I will explain with the help of this example.

1. Amyra, a fourteen-year-old girl is about 15 kg overweight. One day, she sees an inspiring dance recital and feels an intense desire to become a dancer. As she starts practising, she realizes she has a flair for it. She practises hard, imagines herself to be a graceful dancer,

defines herself as one, and after two years of intense work and 18 kg lighter, she becomes a great dancer.
2. Shanaya, another fourteen-year-old, is also about 15 kg overweight. She likes coding and is Amyra's friend. When the whole school starts talking about Amyra's grace as a dancer, Shanaya's mom asks her why is it that she can't dance like Amyra? Shanaya tries a lot. She imagines herself to be a great dancer and gives it her time and effort. But her natural love for coding keeps coming back and interrupting her thought process. One day, tired of not being able to finish a loop, she falls and sprains herself. Free of the pressure of going to the dance class, Shanaya breathes a sigh of relief. Her mom feels guilty.

This entire process of imagining and becoming something you want has a lot to do with 'your source wiring'.

Becoming what you're thinking about—based on some momentary influence—may not necessarily be right for you. Because that influence will wear off with time. The world is replete with teenagers who declared they would be fighter pilots but ended up as bankers.

Becoming what someone else asks you to think about is certainly not right for you either! If you want to become a photographer and your father asks you to be an engineer, you can try your level best to imagine that you will be an engineer.

But if being an engineer is not what you are wired to crave for, there will be heavy internal resistance from your aadi that knows your potential and what you dream to achieve subconsciously. This conflict is different from the 'habituated laziness conflict' we discussed earlier. It is a much deeper

Stage 2: Opt Out Of Being Ordinary (Embracing THECO) • 73

conflict, which will leave you indifferent to the desire for your own growth.

You may become an engineer, but not the best you can be!

Remember, we have discussed that there are two kinds of wiring in the brain—one that exists before birth and one that evolves after birth. The wiring before birth, includes the one connected to your source or aadi or potential and is embedded deep within you before birth.

This source wiring is what we are talking about here. And that's why this part of the book is very important. It is genuinely incredulous to think you can become what you would like to be by simply assuming the feeling in your body of your desires being fulfilled.

My childhood heroes, Steffi Graf and Roger Federer, must have some small speck of 'lawn tennis' within them in the wiring of their source. Sometimes, people who are wired to be alert and athletic tend to excel in several sports.

With their practice, effort and focus, that natural propensity, ingrained deep within their aadi gains the potential to win championships.

Realize that from birth, you already have a small part of what you desire within you. The tragedy is that most of us never find this. Our education and career systems are not built for such deep introspective exploration.

If your wiring is to be a boxer, and you are forced to study aerospace engineering, the fact that it does not feel *natural* to you to be an aerospace engineer could turn out to be the secret of your failure. This could be the cause of much mediocrity in the world.

The movie *Erin Brockovich* is a case in point. It tells the story of how a woman in deep financial trouble, living a mediocre life, rewires herself to believe that she can make a difference. She turns her life around when she sees herself differently and understands what makes her come alive!

Regardless of your desire, regardless of how faithfully and intelligently you follow the practice of positive self-dialogue, if you do not feel programmed from within about what you want to be, you will not be that.

So the next time you attend a career counselling programme and are excited by a new prospect, take some time out for peace. Ask yourself a few questions, and respond honestly.

1. Does it feel natural to you?
2. Does it really feel 'right'—that this is the 'you' that you are deciding to be?

If you've been sedentary for most of your life and you are assuming the feeling of a gymnast, and trying to impress that monologue into your brain, does it feel natural to see yourself as a picture of agile movement?

In the case of the fourteen-year-old Shanaya, if she works on her natural inclination and builds an app she can probably create a new success story.

Summing up, being in tune with your innermost wiring and feeling natural about your desires, is the key to making a successful transition from AIGE to THECO. If you're naturally suitable for something, the chances that you will become that are higher.

The next time you ask yourself an AIGE question, don't make it generic and pointless—end that question with a qualifier-

Replace the 'am I good enough' with

- Does it feel natural for me to aim for Harvard?

- Does it feel natural for me to be a shooter?
- Does it feel natural for me to be a writer?

This will help you evaluate how you really feel. It will give you a sense of what you truly want to become.

Because the light of your true 'nature' that is within you is pure, powerful and immense.

It will shine through, if you allow it to.

As the sun, revealer of all objects to the seer, is not harmed by the sinful eye, nor by the impurities of the objects it gazes on, so the one self, dwelling in all, is not touched by the evils of the world.

—THE UPANISHADS

Making the shift

So your AIGE level, comprising your inner and outer beliefs, tells you what your mind, spirit and body are capable of.

These beliefs inspire your actions, which leave a trail of your state of mind.

Your concept of yourself is everything that you believe to be true about your inner and outer self. These beliefs have created the life you're now living—at what I'd like to call an ordinary level of awareness. Moving into the extraordinary space that I want you to experience requires you to make a change. To change what you believe is true.

This is an excruciatingly difficult task, and very few people are eager or willing to take it on.

The struggle of every human mind is to believe that they're worth everything the universe has to offer.

The very purpose of writing this book is to give you some very specific guidance and help in believing that there is a THECO within you that you must activate.

You have to believe that you are more than what your circumstances dictated at that point.

The Upanishads teach us that 'the infinite—free, unbounded, full of joy—is our native state'.

At the THECO level, you are the person who has the capacity to live a very fulfilling life.

Making the shift to THECO involves three distinct steps.

1. Take on new truths and shed old views of what you believe you could achieve.
2. Your concept of yourself includes your beliefs about your limitations. Allow yourself to let go of them.
3. You will at first reject the thought that there is a higher self within you, either harshly or mildly, depending on the amount of conditioning you have absorbed throughout your life. Recognize this resistance.

I'm encouraging you to initiate a habit of choosing thoughts and ideas that support feeling good and powerful, and that elevate you to a higher level of consciousness where your self-concept welcomes your higher self.

Let's recapitulate what we have done till now:

1. Redefine your self-concept by challenging everything that you've held to be true about yourself until now.
2. Be open to evaluating everything you've previously

thought was your shortcoming or weakness.
3. Spend time in meditation/contemplation, accessing the feelings of a plane of higher consciousness; a plane that you cannot explain, like the planets and the stars and the galaxies—even your consciousness and breath itself. In the words of Jiddu Krishnamurthy, 'Meditation is the emptying of the mind of all the things that the mind has put together. You will find that there is an extraordinary space in the mind, and that space is freedom. So you must demand freedom at the very beginning, and not just wait, hoping to have it at the end.'
4. Whenever you're experiencing discomfort or sadness, rather than trying to change the thought behind your emotional state, just put it back onto the never-ending conveyor belt of thoughts, and then select a different thought. Keep doing this until you've selected a thought that allows you to feel good, and you're no longer condemning yourself for creating unhappy thoughts.

When you are making a shift to the THECO level, your actions originate from the realization that you're not stuck unless you want to be.

Now you have reached the point where you will simply allow yourself to imagine that you can create a new and higher concept of yourself.

Your work has just begun.

And your new inspired self will take a new set of actions and leave behind the evidence of a new you—a new software within you which has been programmed to respond in a new way!

Making peace with the unknown

When you opt out of the ordinary, you begin to appreciate and accept the unknown, and make peace with it.

Because there is no rational explanation of THECO except that you owe it to yourself.

In the new state of THECO, your actions produce a new body of results which leave a new trail of evidence that validate your transformation to enable you to reach your highest self.

Can you answer these questions, derived from Swami Vivekananda's thoughts that we discussed earlier, before you move to the next step?

The seed comes out of the tree; it does not immediately become a tree, but has a period of inactivity, or rather, a period of very fine unmanifested action.

What is this un-manifested action?

The seed has to work for some time beneath the soil. It breaks into pieces, degenerates as it were, and regeneration comes out of that degeneration.

Can you allow your present self to degenerate to allow a new form of you to regenerate?

Everything that you do or think or feel, every part of your conduct or behaviour, every movement—all is caused and therefore not free.

So how can you 'cause' what you want?

> *If you do not change direction,*
> *You may end up where you're heading.*

—LAO TZU

12

Stage 3: Activate Your Imagination

> *When the five senses and the mind are stilled,*
> *when the reasoning intellect rests in silence,*
> *then begins the highest path.*
>
> KATHA UPANISHAD

As the Creator created you, so do you create your future. And you are dependent on one thing above all—your own imagination. When you operate at the THECO level, you realize that the your greatest gift is your imagination. Within your magical inner realm is the capacity to live your dream life. Here, in your imagination, lies the greatest power you will ever know.

> *Why do you stay in prison*
> *when the door is so wide open?*
>
> —JALALUDDIN RUMI

Remember that your imagination is yours and yours alone. Never ever allow anyone else to decide who you can or can't become to cast a cloud on your dream or pollute your imagination. This is your territory. Mark it. Like the kings of yore used to guard their forts, construct 'impregnable barriers' at all entrances to your imagination.

Imagination is part of your aadi

All that we see around ourselves was once only imagined. Hence, our existence today was, at some point, a part of the Creator's imagination.

Imagination is an intrinsic part of your aadi. It has always existed there, creating as it went along. Imagination is fundamental.

And it is one of the most powerful tools you have from where you are to get where you want to be.

During my graduation years, I remember picturing in my head that I would somehow get to go away from the toxic environment that was my home. I wanted to get away so badly that I actually created an alternative in my mind. And higher studies was the only option.

Soon enough, I was in Pune.

And believe me, given my circumstances back then, you would know that I had no power or money to make this happen. Raised in a house where staying out of home beyond

7 p.m. wasn't allowed, getting permission to go to a new city and living there was nothing short of a miracle.

Let's begin with understanding how we can actualize things. Whenever you start any sentence with 'I am', make sure you say something that you wish to create.

Hold this image steadfast in your mind. Don't become restless and impatient after five days and say, 'I'm thinking positive all the time! Why isn't anything good happening to me?'

Remember, what the Atharva Veda says: 'It takes time for a fruit to mature and acquire sweetness and become eatable; time is a prime factor for most good fortunes.'

Hold a positive image of what you want to actualize steadfast in your mind and never let go.

Believing in that ego-driven idea of God as someone who likes sycophants, plays favourites and will punish you if you displease him is pure trash.

Gently remind yourself by acknowledging and applying the active presence of the aadi within you.

As one with your source, which has created so much, you too can create anything.

Your aadi and your imagination

The greatest gift you were ever given was the gift of your imagination. Within your magical inner realm is the capacity to live your dream life.

Here in your imagination lies the greatest power you will ever know. It is your domain for creating the life that you desire, and the best part of it is that you are the emperor of this kingdom with all of the inherent powers to rule your kingdom as you desire.

Look around you.

Everything that you can experience with your hands or your senses was once in someone's imagination. From the mobile phone to the light bulb to the airplane in which I have written some of these chapters, the potent power of your imagination is the great truth that you must come to realize for yourself.

All the mental monologues that have not served you so far need to be edited and replaced.

Once you're connected to your source, you will naturally know your power, opt out of being ordinary and then use this imagination to replace what does not serve you.

In order for something to get into this world where things exist and are proved, they must first be placed firmly in your imagination.

Without your imagination as the reason for future creations, the process of creativity is halted. You have this great power within you. It is a power that is virtually unlimited and it has been given to you as your birthright.

The only belief system that truly serves you is the one in which you love yourself and consider yourself in perfect harmony with your imagination—and believe that it can generate whatever you want or desire. Because you are aadi and when you love yourself, you love the Creator and everything that he has created.

What our ancient texts say about imagination

There is much modern-day emphasis on imagination, but I went back to my fountainhead and started looking for references.

Is it true that by believing passionately in something that does not yet exist, we create it?

We have already established that nothing comes from nothing.

Interestingly, the Upanishads don't say much about imagination per se, in the strictest sense of the word. A Sanskrit word that comes close to mean imagination is kalpana.

I did find some unflattering references over time.

For instance, the Katha Upanishad tells us that virtual objects exist only during kalpana-kaala that is, during the period of imagination owing to avidya, which means ignorance.

The Brihadaranya Upanishad speaks of kalpana as a fictitious view.

Clearly, imagination wasn't held in high esteem. In fact, a book titled the *Introduction to Indian Mysticism* refers to how kalpana was dismissed as a false superimposition on account of ignorance.

The Rig Veda, however, comes to our rescue here. It says, 'Desire links non-being to being.'

The very act of desire implies 'imagining' something that doesn't exist right now.

Imagination therefore is fundamental.

The Bhagwad Gita establishes the point further: 'They alone see truly who see the Lord the same in every creature, who see the deathless in the hearts of all that die.'

Now to see your Creator in all beings most certainly requires imagination.

Imagining things to be a certain way can help you create a world where there is peace and tolerance.

It is your belief that creates things.

I have 'created' experiences in my life and I would encourage you to do the same.

As a child, I had a father I could not depend on at all.

Unfortunately, that defined how uncertain I felt about myself and my future. Today, I have a life partner whom I can depend on blindly. He is a very reassuring, rooted, supportive and joyous presence in my life.

My entreaty to you is that whatever doesn't exist in your life is what you have not sufficiently desired.

I am typing this text on a laptop, which was once someone's imagination only—till they found the tools to make it.

The Atharva Veda says, 'Life without goodness, good thoughts, good actions and good words is like the sky in the night without the moon or stars.'

Remember this, as the Creator created you, so you create your future.

Can you explain your existence? Why do you try to explain anything else around you? Of course, there's the Big Bang theory, but it is complex and requires imagination to understand. But I am willing to accept that someone has made sense of it all. Often, you will be faced with a question you cannot answer. Don't fret. Acceptance is greater than disdain for what you do not fully comprehend.

If I am always in the present, then how will I imagine a future for myself?

This is an important question I had asked myself. While I believe in the power of imagination, Buddhist monk Bodhidharma, the founder of Chan Buddhism in China, which came to be known as Zen in Japan, preaches about the need to become fully aware, here and now.

Additionally, having read and loved spiritual teacher Eckhart Tolle's advice, on 'being in the now', I was caught in a dilemma, between focusing on my present and imagining my future.

The Vedas say: 'The Great Breath goes forth and returns again. As it proceeds outwards, objects, worlds and men appear; as it recedes all disappear into the original source.'

When you focus on your breath, you focus entirely on the present moment.

Living fully and authentically in the present moment gives us profound peace and clarity. Your entire experience of the universe is to be had in this present moment and in all that it has to offer.

How will you follow Bodhidharma's Zen, be in the present and at the same time believe that the universe will answer your every command in the future?

The present and the future together?

It is important to address this dilemma.

There are two words we have to understand to move forward—judgement and acceptance.

What is the meaning of being in the present?

It is mindfulness.

Going back to my childhood, being mindful was realizing that there are only two rotis in the dabba when I came home very hungry, eating them, enjoying their flavour as I ate, being grateful for them and moving on to the next activity.

I was grateful for all the hard work my mom was putting in. I was not judging my reality—or complaining. I was in acceptance mode.

But what if I came home, realized that there were only two rotis in the dabba and started complaining? Why only two rotis? Why aloo curry again? Why not paneer? Why not samosa? Why not anything else for a change?

The feeling of not having doesn't stop here. By now, your negative imagination is activated. You start judging your present—'look at my sad reality. My life sucks!'

In short, when you express dissatisfaction in your present, your imagination makes you miserable. You sow the seeds of unhappiness by comparing yourself constantly with others.

Remember what Nagarjuna said, 'All things exist only in relation to another.'

Essentially, you create a feeling of 'I don't have', and 'I am not the universe's Chosen One in that moment'. Your THECO goes out of the window.

That's being non-mindful.

In contrast, when you cultivate a non-judgemental awareness of the present, it allows you to embrace the THECO mindset.

Practise mindfulness. When you can accept what is in your present moment, you will be happier, more secure and will be able to welcome your positive visualization into existence. You will be accepting of your own weaknesses.

Anchoring awareness in the here and now reduces the kinds of impulsiveness and thoughtless reactivity that creates the real-time problems that we see around us, like depression, binge eating and attention problems.

Mindful people are less attached to labels and definitions of themselves. Hence, they fight less to prove their point, are more accommodating and less defensive. They have the wisdom to believe that all creations are equal and that all are from the same source.

The Upanishads say this best: 'Ahimsa is the natural way once we know that all is one, all are God, all are connected.'

All know the way; few actually walk it.

BODHIDHARMA

Imagining your way to THECO

THECO is the highest possible level you can reach in terms of self-belief.

Imagine you're in a time machine. You have to:

1. Delete personal history of failures that you play in a loop, again and again in your life. These include all the negative talk and experiences that you have heard overtime.
2. Energize your imagination. Write down what kind of person you'd like to be.
3. Ruthlessly eliminate any thoughts/doubts which come in the way of your higher vision of yourself.

You have to decide that you will explore rather than resist your higher powers. You will realize that there is a list of miracles that you take for granted every day. The sun rises to support you. The air has oxygen to support you life. There's free water around you.

These are things beyond your reach.

Because the ride from where 'you are' to where 'you want to be' is meant to be taken on the magic carpet of your imagination.

When you take charge of your imagination, you take 100 per cent ownership of your own improvement. Because the real power within you starts revealing itself. You can then trust your imagination to deliver.

In the words of Adi Shankaracharya, 'The soul appears to be finite because of ignorance. When ignorance is destroyed, the self which does not admit of any multiplicity truly reveals itself by itself: like the sun when the clouds pass away.'

You are infinite. You are powerful.

Imagination is incomplete without action

So far, we have come to this point: Do not let your imagination be restricted to the current conditions of your life, or what I call 'being obsessed with what is'.

Your imagination is unlimited, and if you have opted for an ordinary level of living, then it is time to opt out.

Needless to say, imagination has a steadfast companion called action.

The Vedas have a striking lesson for us here. These texts place a lot of emphasis on rituals. These rituals are divided into a thousand different ways such as meditation, austerities, sacrifices and rites and ceremonies like wedding rituals, digging ponds for the public, in social work, sanskaras like marriage, state affairs, social life, poetry, etc.

What is the goal of all these?

For a moment, observe that the Vedas ask us to keep ourselves busy with action.

The rationale of those times was that the senses are incapable of perceiving the self. Hence, to attain our true 'one' reality', also called the self, we need to discipline our mind in various ways because an idle mind does not easily remain fixed on our goal. So it is only by performing outward functions that we will gain the wisdom and maturity to turn our focus inwards.

These rituals were the actions prevalent in those times. Feel free to choose a different set of actions that stop your mind from wandering all over the place.

Understand that everything that you have believed in has gotten you to precisely the point where you are now. If you want to elevate your life and change anything about it, then you have to change what you have, up to this point in your life, believed to be true about yourself that has landed you where you are. You have to 'direct' your wandering mind towards purposeful action—action that takes you towards your goals.

Here's what you need to do:

1. In your imagination, replace the thought of 'I will one day be in a better place', with 'I am already in my mind where I intend to be'. Can you feel this emotion?
2. Your imagination has to accept the idea that anything placed there isn't for a future experience, but represents your reality—right here, right now. You have to start feeling it *now* to be able to live it.

What you listen to from others is what your ears hear. That is external appreciation, criticism or validation.

But the most powerful conversation happens between your ears, in your mind. You can hear that conversation louder than any other. That's internal self-worth. That's where your imagination takes root. Hence, even on your worst day, don't forget to love yourself.

Aham asmi, Aham Bramhasmi.

Listen to this.

Your *aham asmi* and *aham brahmasmi* coexist beautifully with each other.

Aham asmi means that I exist.

Aham brahmasmi means that the core of my being is the ultimate reality, the root and ground of the universe, the source of all that exists.

Sample two of the problems we began the book with:

- Religious conflicts
- Terrorism

These problems are ample evidence that we misuse our imagination and create scenarios such as:

1. My religion is greater than yours.
2. My ideology is greater than yours.

3. I have something to prove to others.

The misuse of imagination begins with the small things and becomes a habit over time.

Start paying attention to general conversations around you and you will be astounded by how incredibly prevalent the misuse of imagination is.

Sample these:

1. Things never work out for me.
2. I always make silly mistakes in my exams.
3. I have health problems all the time.
4. My husband never listens to me.
5. I am not important enough.

These are classic cases of stupid uses of imagination.

People at peace with themselves simply never imagine what they don't wish to have as their reality. Because their *aham asmi* and their *aham bramhasmi* are both true.

You exist and are part of the universe that exists. You must use your imagination positively.

Now here's where you need to put pen to paper and jot these things down:

1. *Never* place into your imagination any thought that you would not want to materialize.
2. *Never* allow your imagination to be contaminated by ideas about how your life used to be. You need faith in your power to make *the non-existent* your reality. Just because you haven't experienced the magic of the non-existent appearing in your daily life is no reason to poison your imagination with the thoughts that got you where you are now or have been for most of

your life. 'I can't help it', 'I've always been that way', are statements indicating how you have used your imagination in the past.
3. Your imagination can undergo a complete overhaul. Replace the old ideas of 'I have always been this way' or 'It is my nature', with 'I am capable', 'I am strong', 'I am wealthy', 'I am healthy', 'I am happy'.

Whenever you use your imagination in the direction of what you don't want, stop and notice it. Choose a different picture to pursue.

In the lines of the fortieth verse of the *Tao Te Ching*, written by Chinese philosopher Lao Tzu, whom we have quoted earlier in this book as well, is the ultimate tribute to the power of imagination:

'Being is born of non-being.'

Your imagination, when aligned with the highest principles of your highest self, is your Creator at work.

We can say with certainty that the Creator must not have intended to taint the beauty of the world with depression, suicides, wars and religious conflicts.

Living from this realization, it is almost difficult to fathom why the world would have problems at all!

The problems that we have created in the world are simply because we have not understood how powerful our imagination is.

Your imagination, your ability to visualize something, is like a Bramhastra—a potent weapon.

Look at the problems as evidence of this malaise, and make the shift. It won't be easy and it won't be quick because there is a gap between you imagining something positive and then waiting for the thing to materialize.

Remember that your imagination is your own farm. If you plant sunflower seeds, you will get sunflowers. If you do not tend to your imagination and let weeds grow, of what use is mere degree-based education?

Let your spiritual education begin.

Another way to understand THECO

Here's one of the best ways to explain what THECO actually means.

From the time we are born, there are abundant spirits to guide us, but none of them can share our journey with us. We take our first breath by ourselves. And we take our last breath alone.

Somewhere in-between, in the span of time that we call our lifetime, we expect external intervention to help us become more fulfilled. That's like asking someone else to do our breathing for us?

You have to do your own breathing and your own rewiring. No one else will ever recognize the deep-seated auto-programmed responses we give to situations, our sticky bad habits and proceed to rewire us.

This is something we have to do ourselves.

We are born, live and leave this life entirely on our own. We choose where to go and who to meet. What to accept and what to return.

If someone offers you the gift of 'abuse', or makes you feel small, do you accept it or say 'No, thank you?'

Buddha famously said that you don't have to accept every abuse someone throws at you.

Protect the doors to your mind at all costs. No one else

can ever live a single moment of our lives for us or think a single thought for us. That we must do for ourselves.

And to do it with warmth, self-love and affection is the essence of THECO. Do it from the space of being The Chosen One. You have to ignore everything that doesn't truly serve you, such as anger, jealousy, doubt and the opinions of others.

In the words of Jalaluddin Rumi: 'You are a manuscript of a divine letter. Look inside yourself; everything that you want, you are already that.'

The idea of loving yourself is not a borrowed notion. It's a self-activated state of being.

Interpret everything that happens as a glorious opportunity, to learn from or to live with.

Rumi's words sound more like a to-do technology manual than like a philosophy when it comes to establishing your THECO.

Sample this, 'Who could be so lucky? Who comes to a lake for water and sees the reflection of moon?

And this…

'You were born with wings.

You are not meant for crawling, so don't.

You have wings.

Learn to use them and fly.'

13

Stage 4: Master Your Emotions

Wheresoever you go, go with all your heart.

—CONFUCIUS

You are now at the fourth stage. You have learnt to be one with your Creator, opted out of being ordinary and learnt about the power of your imagination.

It is time now to consciously connect with your body. Practise tuning into how your body is feeling. Notice areas of tension or stress.

What you are visualizing with your imagination, think about how it would feel, to achieve it. Tune into your emotion and welcome that new reality into your life today.

Change your emotion, change your life

After all the emphasis on imagination, note this. It is not enough to merely imagine a future that you want.

In order to actually bring this experience to life, you have to bring into your reality the emotions that are associated with that 'imagination'.

Please realize the enormous implications this statement has for you.

Become aware of the importance of 'feeling the experience' and its crucial role in advancing you from someone who merely *has* wishes, to *living out* your wishes in your present life.

So here's your creative process:

1. Have an idea.
2. Invite the emotion of already having it in your life.
3. Live the idea.

'Feeling' an experience is very different from studying it academically.

In order to learn something intellectually, you engage in the practice of mental discipline: studying, researching, memorizing facts, cogitating, participating in discussions and seeking expert opinions. Ultimately, you draw conclusions about what you've been analysing.

Knowing something spiritually is a different matter altogether because you must experience it; there is no other way.

Remember that you cannot simply *think* your way to a new awareness. Your feelings play more of a role in your life than you realize.

You may imagine that you're the chosen one, but unless you feel the warm protection and liberation of the emotion that arises from being THECO, it is challenging to manifest the consequences of that feeling.

The Rig Veda says it beautifully:

'Sages discovered this link of the existent to the non-existent, having searched in the heart with wisdom.'

Your 'emotions' and the strength with which you feel them connect your present to your future.

Let's say that again: Your 'emotions' and the strength with which you feel them connect your present to your future.

You have this incredible power to take a thought that is in your imagination, live from that place in your daily life, then experience in your body exactly how that feels and stay with this feeling.

Your feelings happen in your body, where you live and breathe. How you feel on a daily basis adds up to your experience of life. These feelings flow from the thoughts you place in your imagination, and you are free to select any thought you desire. Your *feelings* are the tools you have for experiencing your subconscious mind and making it your material world reality.

The subconscious mind cannot make a distinction between what you feel as a result of your daily life experiences today and what you feel as a result of what you have placed into your imagination as a future desire.

Your mind has the power of the universe within it. It is far too powerful to be wasted. Hence, you have to keep tabs on what feelings you are associating with and the wishes you have placed in your imagination. Because whatever they are, you will see the universe aligning with them to provide experiences that match up with what you have impressed upon this universal subconscious mind.

Work with *aham sukhi,* or I am happy, as the base.

Understanding your subconscious mind

I am only going to scratch the surface of this, but feel free to read other experts to gain understanding about the subconscious mind.

The conscious mind is just a fraction of the total capacity of the human brain and is essentially whatever you are currently aware of and focused upon. It sleeps when you sleep, it is more logical and is focused in terms of activity on the left hand side of the brain for the majority of people.

Your subconscious mind is illogical, irrational, non-analytical. It is the storage place of all your memories, emotions and habits. Your subconscious is hard at work forming logical patterns of association (habits, beliefs and emotions) that help you to survive. It has a powerful ability to direct your focus.

The subconscious mind is the womb of creation. It accepts as true what you feel is true. Your feelings determine your reality because they're impressed on the subconscious.

For example, if you're consciously feeling poor, unattractive or lonely and entertaining this idea in your imagination, in a graphic expressive way, you will be offered experiences by the one universal subconscious mind that will match what you're feeling and make it true.

If you put the seed of *failure* into the subconscious and feed it with feeling that way, it will reproduce failure.

If you plant the seed of *disease* into your subconscious mind by feeling this way in your body, it will augment a disease for you.

If you plant the seed of *being unattractive* into your subconscious mind by feeling miserable, it will cultivate and produce misery for you.

Have you seen girls and boys who do not fit in your definition of 'classic' beauty, but who are so confident that they are labelled strikingly attractive?

Their mental monologue is *I look so good*, and the universe responds that way.

As a result, when we casually state, 'No matter what I do, I just can't seem to look attractive enough to get the right guy's/girl's attention,' our subconscious mind says, 'Okay, I'll do what you're telling me to do. I'll make sure you don't get the right guy's/girl's attention.'

Your subconscious mind unleashes its powerful control over your mental and physical self to achieve the result it was told to accomplish. Hence, it is critical that you don't let your emotions read from your troubles, difficulties or illnesses. They're in your past and you must let them go.

Your subconscious mind accepts all the feelings associated with your troubles as your request to it. Your subconscious mind works day and night to make sure that you become precisely the person you have described yourself to be.

If you have conditioned yourself to believe that you can't stick to an exercise regimen, you can be sure that your subconscious mind will make *sure* that no exercise will work for you—at least not for long! Your subconscious can only do for you what you (and others) tell it to.

We are all victims of an unconscious habit of programming ourselves in the same wrong way as did our parents, friends and others around us. And right now, at this moment, each of our subconscious minds is working to make sure we become just what those tens of thousands of negative directives programmed us to be.

This is not an intellectual exercise—this is about how you feel.

Remember what the Rig Veda points out: 'Desire links non-being to being.'

Desire is an emotion.

It is the link between what you seek and your present. The

more thoughts and actions you practise around your new 'I am', the more the subconscious mind will react in kind until eventually it will act in generous ways out of a new habit that you've created. You have the power to impress upon the subconscious mind any 'I am' of your choosing. Three steps to work in tune with your powerful subconscious mind.

1. Practise feeling a thought that you have inserted into your imagination. Remember that a feeling is what you feel in your body as you think what you would like to manifest or who you would like to become.
2. Close your eyes and experience what that feels like in your body. Work with the sensations—let them build and become stronger.
3. Act in line with this feeling, for example, if you'd like to feel generous, then tell yourself, 'I am a generous person'. Give something away in a spirit of generosity, even if it's only a small coin or a word of encouragement. Make it a habit so you can re-inforce the feeling.

Whatever we plant in our subconscious mind and nourish with repetition and emotion, will one day become a reality.

—EARL NIGHTINGALE

To master your subconscious, start thinking in terms of 'I

am' rather than 'I will' and 'I have', rather than 'I will have'.

Because the 'I will' establishes a lack of something—that 'I am not'.

So change your 'I will become desirable someday', to 'I am desirable'. Start feeling the emotions of the warm glow of attention that is pointed in your direction.

You will in time impress your subconscious mind with all that it needs in order to match your desires with your reality.

Let's go back to my story for a bit.

2000—Y2K as we called it

In July 1999, Appa died.

In February 2000, I got married.

I asked my partner just one question—'Why me?' He said, 'Because you will make a good mother to my children.'

He asked me the same question and I responded, 'Because you look like the kind of man who will stick around to take care of his children.'

That was that. We knew exactly what we were getting into.

The physical events leading up to my wedding involved one embarrassing ceremony after another, where the meagre means and simple kanjeevarams of my family collided with the designer saris and diamond necklaces of my better half's family.

It was a robotic phase as I went through the motions. Amma and Renu put up their best smiles too. I don't know whether I missed Appa.

Till that point in my life, I had no idea that the dowry system was so prevalent in our country. That men considered it an entitlement, and fathers of daughters gladly gave it too, and prepared for it actively from the time of their daughters' birth! Consequently, I met with several people who either gave me the 'poor girl' condescending stare, or the 'we cannot believe this is happening' iciness.

There was a phase where I couldn't decide what to make of the people I was getting introduced to. Some of them had already made up their mind to be nice to me, while some had decided otherwise.

As it happens with marriages between unequals, there's usually one tough nut who holds the fragile equations together and says, 'I don't care what she brings, or doesn't, but the show must go on.' That was my mother-in-law.

She received her share of incredulous stares.

But my mother-in-law was ardently devoted to her son and his happiness and nothing else mattered. I didn't know it then, but my mother-in-law was going to play a major part in shaping the couple of decades that lay before me.

As I moved into another home and new surroundings, I wasn't prepared for the massive cultural conflict.

Surviving ambiguity would be the biggest problem.

There are some of the questions commonly asked of me in the first three months of marriage:

1. What can you cook?
2. What did your father really do?
3. Do you know how much 'stuff' your sister-in-law brought home?

The fact that I was from a family without money to give as dowry was reiterated in a hundred different ways. By everyone that I encountered!

And for some weird reason, almost everything in my house

was either brought in as dowry by my mother-in law's family or my sister-in-law's family. At least that's what I was told.

Questions asked of me in the next six months:

1. When are you planning a baby?
2. Do you have any wealthy relatives at all?
3. Can you make aloo curry?

Suffice to say that I felt so un-valued and poor, that even my great love affair with my Creator, my THECO, was floundering.

As a piece of advice, note this—in a joint family, you marry the family. You spend only 10 per cent of the time with your man!

I often tried reacting and retaliating. I had topped biochemistry in my TYBSC and was an MBA graduate. I could earn good money and would've probably been in a cushy job in the US if I had not chosen to get married.

But mouthing these realities was like selling ice to an Eskimo. Only the bank balance seemed to matter. And all these conversations always happened when the man of the house was not around.

Initially, I decided to complain religiously, every evening.

But the entire idea of reliving a depressing day, again in the night with my narration, was itself very uninviting.

I was relentlessly thrust into situations where I had to make very difficult choices.

Apart from patriarchy and gender imbalance in the roles that men and women are supposed to play, there were some set patterns. Men gave women money to run the house, and in turn took their voice away.

Women would do their share of the work at home and they were expected to dress up in the finest jewellery and clothes while stepping out.

To add to this, there was a continuous emphasis on superstitious beliefs that I was exposed to that made no sense to me at all.

Sample these—don't buy leather on Saturdays; no haircuts on Thursdays; no eating papad on the day when you're travelling; no returning from your mom's house on Sundays—the list was endless.

There was no dearth of external pundits who would somehow get into my house and make loony predictions. After about thirty minutes of gaining my father-in-law's trust by revealing some information that they could've easily had, they would con him into another elaborate ritual and ask for some dakshina.

I also realized that in joint families, the way to avoid conversations of importance was to throw a tantrum. Initially I had toyed with the idea of using my education to manage some part of the family business. I soon realized that the mere suggestion would be received with rage, judgements, disdain and mockery.

I had to step out and achieve a future for myself. My belief systems and education did not allow me to imagine that I would be financially dependent on someone else.

I began with a small job but I wasn't happy. All my education, all my erudition, everything I had learnt, it seemed, was lost on a family that somehow measured everything with inherited money. As if no one was capable of building anything substantial or new.

So I continued working quietly and brought myself some 'creative' time outside of the 'cloud of discouragement' I faced with the family.

And it was a 'cloud'—there was no one villain—but an overall atmosphere where one irrational thought after another, one superstition after another, and one fear after another played out constantly, making for a very unsavoury regressive environment.

One thing had changed for good though; now, when I stepped outside, this whole, 'what does your father do', had now given way to 'what does your husband do?'

And I was thrilled to finally have an answer. 'He is a very driven entrepreneur.'

As my marriage turned a year, a new question had emerged. When was I going to produce a son?

March 2002: My daughter

The birth of my beautiful daughter in March 2002 inspired me to overcome the depths of deprivation my mind had succumbed to.

Looking at the little dependent 2.4-kg bundle of joy, Dheeraj and I now had the motivation to ensure we would improve the quality of conversations that she would be exposed to when growing up

Look at this brilliant verse from the Rig Veda:

'The human body is the temple of God. One who kindles the light of awareness within gets true light.'

Yes, the light of awareness was missing at home.

There was a strain of not producing a boy all around me. Some people I encountered were so flagrant in their blindness that within the first six months of my daughter's birth, I was asked about when would I try for a second child!

Strangely enough, women who had sons as firstborns could

get away with 'My family is complete'. How did that make any sense? Girl or boy, a sibling is a sibling!

Apparently, I wasn't qualified to say that because I had given birth to a daughter!

I realized there was no pleasing those who gave themselves reason to be displeased. Somewhere, I resolved that I had to find the courage to live from my THECO again, and build my future.

I called upon my highest self to ignore anything that didn't serve me. But the highest self took some time to come around.

Mastering my emotions

Five years into my marriage, I was mastering ambiguity, mastering anger, mastering the feeling of being 'incomplete', 'unworthy' and desperately trying to cope in whatever way I could—that was my story.

The funniest incidents in hindsight were about 'pilferage'— whenever something used to go missing from the household, money or valuables—I was among the suspects, along with the many servants in the household.

I was the one without money, remember? Things were so low that they couldn't go any lower.

Today, when I look back, I realize that everything that happened to me after my marriage taught me to master my emotions—I had to develop such thick skin to the universal 'cloud' of aversion and assumed disrepute, that nothing could affect me anymore.

Yes, self-talk looks easy in theory—you must imagine this, visualize that, let go of what doesn't serve you, and basically inhabit some new world that you create for yourself!

Doing it in reality, when you're going through deep distress, requires another level of resolve altogether.

In so many ways my MBA degree wasn't a patch on this intense lesson in emotional management.

Year after year, occasion after occasion, I met with belligerent male chauvinism, patriarchy and women being judged by the extent of their dowries.

I realized that I had lapsed completely into negative mental monologues.

Oh poor me!

Where am I stuck!

Somewhere along the way, I started hating my life and the people around me. I was operating from a place of negativity, hatred and everything I did not want.

O mankind! I ordain for you to have concordance in your heart, unanimity in your minds and freedom from hatred. Every one of you ought to love one another in every way just as the cow loves the calf just born.

—ATHARVA VEDA

December 2005

My son was born.

Thankfully! And I mean it as a sigh of relief.

Driven to desperation by an emotionally regressive environment, I had consumed 'the extract' of banyan tree leaves, juice of some potent seeds, and what not in this elusive quest for a male offspring.

I was 'supposedly' delivered into nirvana. As far as the family 'cloud' was concerned, my life's biggest reason for existence, bearing a son, was now complete.

But while I was now 'celebrated' for being a mother to a son, I found myself abhorring the structure that celebrated such abominable concepts.

And while I adore my bundle of joy, my son, and love him as much as I love my daughter, I wasn't willing to join the 'patriarchy brigade'. I wanted to take a stand against how women were treated at home, the rituals we were expected to perform and the fact that nothing progressive or positive was ever discussed at home except when guests would come home and we were expected to laugh till our jaws hurt.

Do you know what is even more toxic than physical violence? Emotional violence.

April 2009 to October 2011

A decision was made to walk away from what was my home.

All four of us.

As two friends who met during MBA, Dheeraj and I had a very different level of mutual respect for each other.

I had given this home ten years and something inside

me wasn't willing to sacrifice a single more day of my life to regressive thought processes.

So when I decided to leave, Dheeraj agreed to be supportive of my decision. This was the hardest thing for us to do as a family with two small children—to move into a tiny rented apartment without the army of servants and household help we were used to.

In hindsight, though unsavoury and full of real challenges, those thirty months (2.5 years) helped me put my entire life in perspective.

1. I became dead serious about my work. I did not give myself the option to sit and cry.
2. I rebuilt the entire framework of my dialogues within myself. There were days when I would recite my plans to build a happy family. You see, when you talk to yourself out loud, you force yourself to put your thoughts into words. Does it sound foolish? Perhaps, but I encourage you to try it in solitude. It will help you to clarify your thinking on any subject and your goals will become much more specific.
3. I started telling myself, aloud, 'We are good as a family. We are blessed and will have access to every joy.'
4. I took counsel with myself. All of us have a pretty good friend within us, who has been waiting to hear from us, and who is fully vested in us. I used to evaluate my plans for a better future.

I think the shock of us actually 'leaving' and not being able to take 'emotional abuse' (that was me), took some time to hit the family. They never believed we would take such a drastic step.

Because the common belief is 'where will she go?'

Daughters-in-laws stay put, stay quiet and grin and bear it! Stay in the ordinary. Because the idea is that people find it so tough to leave their comfort zone, that they stay in the ordinary.

And then something phenomenal happened! My in-laws, who kept visiting us in our meagre rented apartment suddenly started looking older and more frail. Their eyes would ache to see the children.

One look at them, and I thought, Were these the people who created the 'cloud of contempt' that I had experienced all along? They seem so harmless now!

Were they the problem anyway? Or was it everyone else too who used to walk in and walk out with fears, opinions, diktats and third-rate suggestions for a whole new derogatory ritual?

Suddenly, my in-laws seemed victims too of what their parents and peers and their 'claustrophobic' circumstances had handed down to them. They did not know another way to think than to celebrate male children and think that women belong in the kitchen.

As I said, those thirty months gave me the breathing space to rewire my mind, and forgive wholeheartedly. We gave up our rented home and went back in October 2011. There was one big difference—I was made to feel valued and welcome—for the first time.

As long as man is overpowered by the darkness of ignorance, he is the slave of Nature and must accept whatever comes as the fruit of his thoughts and deeds. When he strays into the path of unreality, the sages declare that he destroys himself because he who clings to the perishable body and regards it as his true self must experience death many times.

—THE UPANISHADS

Concentration: A tool to master your emotion

I was back home, a home I had set foot in as a bride, and received with positive emotion.

What we needed to do now, as partners, was concentrate on the work we had done over the past thirty months, and consolidate the experiences our extended family too could have.

Concentration is a key process

You have to cut out all the noise and distractions. These could be from your friends, relatives or colleagues who claim to know you very well and dissuade you from making any changes that they think might cause them to feel inadequate or uncomfortable.

You have to say no to going out late at night and choose the discipline of early mornings. You have to choose patience over instant results, perseverance over recommendations, every single time.

Through determination and unabashed intention, you can begin the process of assuming the feeling of a new reality, living in it, and feeling it in your body.

Concentration is a razor sharp focus on the omnipresence and omnipotence of your Creator.

Never let your attentiveness to what you are manifesting, be sidetracked by external pressures of any kind.

Whatever you place in your imagination and feel is present, will become a part of your daily life, suddenly appearing in many of your conversations and activities.

Television, movies, internet tidbits and news reports on the same subject will make their way to your consciousness. When you think of buying a new car, notice how you start seeing that same car all around you.

I am asking you now to ignore every bit of information that's directed at you if it in any way contradicts the 'I am' you have placed in your imagination. This is particularly relevant when it comes to the data you receive from your own senses. If you feel like you've had a few setbacks recently, feel the emotion of 'I am successful'. Now concentrate on how this emotion makes you feel and discard what your senses tell you.

Stay with your subjective attention, persistently and adamantly proclaiming, 'I am successful'.

You must attach yourself spiritually to what you have placed in your imagination as a future fact, and never allow anyone, anything, any circumstance—no matter how persuasive their case—to alter what you know to be your destiny.

Develop a healthy attitude towards your highest self, your Creator, your aadi, and all that it beckons you to be.

With the triple tools of imagination, emotion and concentration, your Creator will manifest in you.

14

Stage 5: Find Your Values

Pure consciousness is ever present everywhere, yet it is perceived by the eye of wisdom alone: but one whose vision is obscured by ignorance does not see it; as the blind do not see the resplendent sun.
The Meditator, free from impurities, being heated in the fire of knowledge kindled by learning and so on, shines of itself like gold.
Pure consciousness, the Sun of Knowledge that rises in the sky of the heart, destroys the darkness of the ignorance, pervades and sustains all and shines and makes everything to shine.

—ADI SHANKARACHARYA

Having a clear sense of what matters most to you is important. Because even a terrorist can imagine, feel and visualize a 'future'. But your values and your consciousness determine what difference you will make in this world.

What are values?

In life, there will be situations that test your patience, your character and peace of mind. Your values will guide you and shape your priorities and reactions.

For me, they serve as markers to tell me if my life is heading in the right direction and if it is turning out the way I want it to.

When our actions and words are aligned with our values, life is generally good and we feel content, confident and satisfied. When you consider your values in decision-making, you can be sure to keep your sense of integrity and what you know is right, and approach decisions with confidence and clarity.

But when our behaviour doesn't match up with our values, we soon begin to sense an uneasiness that begins to swell and grow inside of us. Our self-worth suffers greatly. We are not able to see ourselves as the shining light of hope and possibility.

That's why, the final step of rescripting your mental monologue involves deep self-introspection.

Because your personal fulfilment will happen only when you align all areas of life, work and relationships around your values, your own definition of success and what is most important to you. This book is about changing your wiring on a permanent basis—and no such permanent change can happen without addressing the values that matter to you.

You have to list down the values—or what I like to refer to as 'rocks'—that matter to you. Because your personal fulfilment is the achievement of life goals which are important to you as an individual, in contrast to the goals of society, family and other collective obligations.

It has very little to do with what others think.

There are happy teachers, unhappy businessmen, happy musicians, unhappy lawyers, happy housewives, unhappy actresses, happy entrepreneurs, unhappy CEOs—it's all part of the game.

Your success is what you think of success to be.

Here's a list of values that you can start working with. Which one of these is dear to you? This is by no means an exhaustive list.

Accountability
Adventurousness
Ambition
Assertiveness
Balance
Belonging
Boldness
Calmness
Cheerfulness
Clear-mindedness
Commitment
Community service
Compassion
Competitiveness
Courtesy
Creativity
Curiosity

Decisiveness
Dependability
Determination
Dharma
Diligence
Discipline
Discretion
Economy
Empathy
Enthusiasm
Equality
Excellence
Excitement
Expertise
Exploration
Expressiveness
Fairness
Faith
Family-orientedness
Fatalism
Fitness
Fluency
Focus
Freedom
Fun
Generosity
Goodness
Grace
Growth
Happiness
Hard Work

Health
Holiness
Honesty
Honour
Humility
Independence
Ingenuity
Inner harmony
Inquisitiveness
Insightfulness
Intelligence
Intellectual pride
Intuition
Joy
Justice
Leadership
Legacy
Love
Loyalty
Making a difference
Mastery
Merit
Obedience
Obsequiousness
Openness
Order
Originality
Patriotism
Perfection
Persistence
Piety

Positivity
Practicality
Punctuality
Prudence
Quality-orientation
Quest of wealth
Reliability
Resourcefulness
Restraint
Self-control
Selflessness
Self-reliance
Sensitivity
Shrewdness
Shyness
Simplicity
Soundness
Strength
Teamwork
Temperance
Thankfulness
Thoroughness
Thoughtfulness
Timeliness
Tolerance
Trustworthiness
Truth-seeking
Understanding
Uniqueness
Unity

Phew! That was a mouthful.

Are you done with ticking the values that you believe are dear to you?

The connect between values and positive thinking

Positive thinking, like motivation, is one of those potentially life-changing concepts. I am sure it may have worked for millions of people.

Positive thinking is an excellent concept that goes a long way towards helping people readjust their thinking and do better in their lives. It is one of the answers to helping us effect a major change in our lives.

However, it can seem superficial. How do you get up one morning and start thinking positive, without undergoing the five steps we are discussing here?

If it is possible for you, it's a good thing. My submission is that positive thinking is just one part of rescripting your life and awakening your capacity and potential.

Positive thinking *should* work for everyone, and make people happy. Look at the World Happiness Index. It identifies six variables to support well-being—income, healthy life expectancy, social support, freedom, trust and generosity.

Let's look at the first one—income. Globally, the richest 1 per cent own 50 per cent of the wealth as per a Credit Suisse report, and in India, the richest 1 per cent corner 73 per cent of the wealth generated in the country as per an Oxfam report.

Clearly, positive thinking can result in far more equitable wealth distribution.

The World Happiness Index also identifies obesity and depression as two major causes for people being unhappy.

Therefore, either many of us are not thinking positively,

or we don't know how to really do it. Because just making a decision to never again think negatively and think positively for the rest of our lives is short-lived. Like we discussed unshackling habits earlier in this book, evolution dictates that the old programming that controls our habits will once again take over.

The new understanding of conquering the world and thinking positive will be 'postponed' the minute something significant comes along.

The decision to be a positive thinker may often be short-lived.

Imagine that your mind is in the middle of a tug of war. Positive thoughts and negative thoughts are pulling your mind in two different directions.

What will determine who wins?

My argument here is that it is your values that will determine which side triumphs.

Many of your values are handed down from your conditioning—and wiring—from your parents, teachers and relatives.

These are some examples of what several of us might have grown up with:

1. Your father was a stickler for timeliness.
2. Your mother liked to keep her house squeaky clean.
3. You grew up in a culture where there was always black money at home and taxes were evaded.
4. Your mother was obese and did not seem to care much about nutrition.
5. There was regular smoking and drinking at home.

Given the above exposure, punctuality, meticulousness,

evasion of taxes, inactivity, permission to drink and smoke, could be the values that are inside different people, fixated in their wiring.

Imagine this scenario.

You grew up in an environment where there was regular smoking and drinking at home. But you resolve to change, and positivity is tugging at you very hard. One Sunday morning at 9, you remove every trace of alcohol from your living room, keep it in the attic and lock it.

I'll give it to my friends; why waste the money, is the explanation you give yourself.

You continue to think positive. *I am free of addiction or bad habits and am living a centred, balanced and a positive life.*

You move around, thinking and feeling positive. A few hours pass by and you haven't really planned anything for the day.

Your friends call. They want to come over and chill. You are happy to allow it.

At 4 p.m. Your friend arrives with four beers. You tell them about your newfound positivity. They laugh in your face and thrust a chilled beer into your hand.

You tell yourself that '*Hey, it's okay. I can start tomorrow.*'

After two beers and some laughs by 7 p.m., you retrieve one more beer from the attic. A few more friends join. One by one, you will begin to bring your old alcohol back into your living room.

Why? Because when you removed the alcohol from your house, you missed out two things—reconfiguring your life around your new set of values and saying no to relapsing to the old set of values.

So if your new values are to stay 'fit and sober and mindful', you have to choose a different set of actions.

First of all, don't keep your alcohol thinking that you'll give it to someone else. Don't pass along your negative mental monologues to someone else. After all, that's how you got it in the first place!

Throw it outside your house. Let the garbage truck take it away.

Now replace your old value—of being okay with alcohol—with a new one.

I'm not okay with casual drinking. Great!

Follow this up with action—go swimming, or play some game, or go running—whatever activity you like.

So when your friend calls at 4 p.m., you will be in a very different frame of mind, not lazing around at home, with nothing to do!

You will be so tired after your activity that you will crash on the bed by 9.30. p.m. You would have missed your friend's call and the binge night that followed.

What I'm saying is that when you decide to remove bad habits from your life, you have to have an immediate, new and positive habit as well as vocabulary to replace the old. Otherwise, you will *always return to* the comfortable, negative habits of the past.

You have to allow your values to dictate a new set of behaviour for you, which will then replace the old ones.

This is how positive thinking will really work. That is the difference between just believing in positive thinking and actually creating it in your life.

However, you need to ensure that positive thinking does not turn into 'wishful thinking'.

You have to throw out the old; it is essential.

But it is also essential to replace the old with the new;

action for action, thought for thought.

The five core values

We have listed many values earlier, but here are my picks—values that can be common for all of us.

Honesty

Honesty promotes openness, empowers us and enables us to develop consistency in how we speak to ourselves and to others. Honesty sharpens our perception and allows us to observe everything around us with clarity. Honesty and its bedfellow, integrity, should be the bedrock of your foundation, as it will define who you are before you even allow others to know more about you.

If you always deal in the truth, you will live your life in far less worry. Your analytical mind is freed up to think of new ideas rather than lies and excuses. Honest intentions in speech and action gain the attention and respect of others.

Confidence

Is confidence a value?

Yes. A major component of confidence is the value you place on yourself. Confidence is about the faith you have in your abilities, the person you are and how you view your most important relationship—the one with yourself. It's a powerful value that gives so much definition to the core of who you are. Your wiring depends on the way you choose to talk to yourself.

Confidence is about self-worth and appraising ourselves

in a positive way. It is our representation of the way we want to be seen and how we want to see ourselves. It has a major impact on our mental monologue.

Diligence

Diligence is about being in 'the arena', showing up and taking action. You have to spend time honing your craft. If you want to paint, or write, then go do that. Start doing it, then learn what it takes to be the best.

You'll improve in skill and realize that repetition is the key to attaining perfection. Keep going and follow the formula of the greats. We need to understand that everyone fails at one point or another. Sometimes, the way we get knocked down is completely out of our control. But we have to respond and we have to rise to the occasion. You'll find persistence and diligence are ingredients that any happy and successful person puts into practice.

Passion

Passion is that which sets your soul on fire. Fire is enthusiasm. It's unbridled passion and excitement for living your life on your terms. Our passion wills us to carry on towards our goals and dreams.

These are the mental and physical actions that fuel us. They put us on a trajectory to the top. Passion causes you to wake up at 6 a.m. and put on your running shoes. It makes you push yourself and feel the exhilaration of exhaustion.

Agile-mindedness

Sometimes we get lost in ourselves. Our own personal worlds consume us and we forget that there are several billion other people on this planet with several billion different experiences and upbringings. We form opinions and become steadfast in them. To be agile-minded is to remove your personal biases and prejudices from any situation and be open to completely immerse yourself in another experience. It asks to remove all the old wiring, all the old software programming and fit in some new ones.

Agile-mindedness is different from open-mindedness, in the sense that it emphasizes on accepting change—with pace, energy and enthusiasm, as opposed to 'giving up' and 'giving in'.

Rescripting your life demands that you unlearn and re-learn, and you need an agile mind to do this.

Why are values such a big deal?

Look at this argument carefully.

The first four steps of rescripting your life with a new, self-assured mental monologue can be done by anybody.

1. Connect to your source.
2. Opt out of the ordinary.
3. Ignite your imagination.
4. Feel the emotion.

Even a terrorist can follow these paths and blow up the world, full of his own crazy unjust imagination and inspiration.

So what will create lasting peace in the world? What is that one factor that determines whether an inspired man becomes a master thief of a Nobel laureate. The fifth step—finding your values—are fundamental to closing this gap.

Going back to the beginning of this book—being unkind to yourself is violent. And whether are not you believe it, it is the cause of all other violence in the world.

When you choose a set of values that do not resonate with your Creator, your source, your aadi, you are being unkind to yourself.

Your values are the defining factor in all the important choices you make. Values play a central role in decision-making.

People attach values to all sorts of things: career, money, possessing material things, love, education and so on. What people consider to be of value, they find worthy of their pursuit.

In short, values are one of the prime motivating factors in human behaviour. They are definitive of our personality. Once we have chosen the set of values that we find most worthy of our pursuit, then our route to achieving them, and the behaviour we must adopt, are pretty much defined.

The values that so define us are usually called our core values. These are basic values that we might be willing to die for, that we would not sacrifice nor abandon.

Patriotism is one such value that has inspired so many people during India's freedom struggle.

These have a massive impact on our mental monologue. When you make an unscrupulous choice based on compromised values, it impacts your self-esteem. Low self-esteem will take you back to the rut of negative mental monologues. This is being unkind to yourself.

Wife-beaters, rapists, paedophiles, sex traffickers, contract killers, etc., are people with the lowest self-esteem. They have no value filters at all, and hence live robotic lives to fulfil their baser needs on a daily basis.

However, when your values are integrity, honesty, etc., you start making the right choices, which enhance your self-image. You learn to say 'no' till the right opportunity comes along.

Believing in yourself impacts your relationship with others.

We often focus on nourishing our bodies with fitness and nutritious food, and forget that to function at our optimal level and experience overall well-being, it is equally important to nourish our minds. Values are high-nourishment food for your mind.

Having a strong set of values puts you in a resourceful frame of mind. This opens up communication with everyone around you.

With this enhanced understanding, take a look at these values and see which one of these is most important to you. Match them with what you have ticked earlier.

You will be surprised by how much more careful you will be this time—now that you're clear about the choices you have made so far in your life. Choose carefully and know that values are not an abstract thing; they define your character.

1. A comfortable life (not too much exertion, limited capacity for risk and experiences)
2. True friendship (long-lasting close companionships over other things)
3. Equality (brotherhood, equal opportunity for all)
4. Family (taking care of loved ones)
5. Freedom (independence, free choice)
6. Inner harmony (freedom from inner conflict)
7. National security (protecting your country against all odds)

8. Salvation (deliverance from sin; eternal life)
9. Respect (self and others, including elders)
10. Social recognition (respect, admiration)
11. Peace (freedom from wars and conflict)
12. Supporting art and culture (being seen as a patron)
13. Community development and philanthropy (community service)
14. Wealth (to afford whatever money can buy)
15. Power (to be able to influence people and outcomes)
16. Privacy (obscurity and non-interference)
17. Devotion to God (deep religious beliefs and practices)
18. Thrill (a stimulating, exciting life free of monotony)

Now evaluate which of these values were responsible for the last ten decisions you took and which of those decisions are you proud of.

If required, feel free to choose a different set of values.

Master catalysts who will help you choose your values

Throughout this book, we have listened to several masters. In the next few pages, to cement your values and help you resolve the dilemma that you will face, I have tried to share the wisdom of three master catalysts—Nagarjuna, Bodhidharma and Sri Aurobindo.

However, as I have said in the beginning of the book, feel free to take inspiration from any of the enlightened ones the world has seen.

Master Catalyst 1: Nagarjuna

After the Buddha himself, if anyone is regarded as an authoritative proponent of Buddhism, it would be Nagarjuna.

Believed to be born in the second century CE, hundreds of years before Swami Vivekananda, he was the first to propose the concept of shunyavada (emptiness), and the idea that the effect is contained within the cause.

Nagarjuna attempted to prove that all things lack essential characteristics and exist only in relation to the conditions surrounding them.

The woman who goes to the kitty party in an Innova is perfectly happy till she learns that someone else has come in a Jaguar.

This comparison will breed despair.

Therefore, everything is relative.

Imagine every argument that you have ever had with your parents or your spouse, and how the fact that someone else—who you think has money or is more privileged—is referenced constantly during the argument.

Since most of those things we call problems are really 'relative' and only *perceived* as problems, the way you look at each of them determines whether they really are problems or not; you need only tell yourself to see them in a better way.

Now, imagine that you remove yourself from these situations where you have to keep comparing yourself to others. Centre yourself to your source and your core and accept who you are fully.

Pick up a purpose and a mindset that is greater than yourself or any other person around you. Feel inspired.

You will find that idle comparisons melt away.

Nagarjuna's sayings are very powerful and resonate even today with modern philosophy. Sample this:

'If you desire ease, forsake learning.

If you desire learning, forsake ease.

How can the man at his ease acquire knowledge?
And how can the earnest student enjoy ease?'

As a lifelong student of rescripting your programming with positive mental monologues, you will have to make some tough choices.

Understand that the journey to THECO and living from your source demands that you will be at 'unease'. But this 'unease' is negligible if you compare it to facing the consequences of what 'negative wiring' will throw at you in life.

So persist and persevere.

Master Catalyst 2: Bodhidharma

'The mind is like the wood or stone from which a person carves an image. If he carves a dragon or a tiger, and seeing it fears it, he is like a stupid person creating a picture of hell and then afraid to face it.'

This is what depression or low self-esteem is all about—imagining the worst.

Bodhidharma is believed to have lived around the sixth century.

Zen has a very interesting origin. The Sanskrit word 'dhyana' for meditation, became the Chinese 'chan' and then the Japanese 'Zen'.

The whole point of Zen is to become fully aware, here and now. To come home to the present moment because this is truly where we live.

Without this 'present state', also explained beautifully by spiritual teacher Eckart Tolle, you cannot make sense of any of the other philosophies outlined in this book.

Living fully and authentically in the present moment gives us profound peace and clarity. Your entire experience of the universe is to be had in this present moment and in all that it has to offer. Zen asks you to 'come to your senses', for when we get lost in thoughts of the past or future, life passes us by.

Here are three thumb rules that can help us understand Zen:

1. Zen sends us looking inside ourselves for enlightenment. There's no need to search outside ourselves for the answers. We can find the answers in the same place that we found the questions.
2. Human beings cannot learn this truth by philosophizing or rational thought, nor by studying the scriptures, taking part in rites and rituals, or many of the other things that religious people do.
3. The first step is to control our minds through meditation.

The beauty of Zen is that it allows space for deep thought and an opportunity to spend time with oneself.

Remember that your mental monologue is a silent one. It includes anything and everything you think about yourself or anything else around you.

To engineer a subtle shift in your attitude to looking at everything in a more positive, productive way is a silent task calling for great inner peace and strength.

When you begin rephrasing your mental monologue from the old to the new, your old programming will try to talk you out of it. By knowing what to expect, you will be ready to confront your habituated old monologues head on, override it and begin building a new habit.

Any student of Zen knows this well—the answers to your problems are within you.

Master Catalyst 3: Sri Aurobindo

Aurobindo Ghose, better known as Sri Aurobindo, came to limelight with his active participation in the freedom struggle against the British in India but he gradually evolved to become a spiritual and yogic guru.

He had great insights into what we call our ability to rise above what we have inherited as our programming or wiring and reboot.

In his words,

- 'The ordinary life is that of the average human consciousness separated from its own true self and from the Divine and led by the common habits of the mind, life and body which are the laws of the Ignorance.'
- 'This is a miracle that men can love God, yet fail to love humanity. With whom are they in love then?'
- 'True knowledge is not attained by thinking. It is what you are; it is what you become.'
- 'If mankind only caught a glimpse of what infinite enjoyments, what perfect forces, what luminous reaches of spontaneous knowledge, what wide calms of our being lie waiting for us in the tracts which our animal evolution has not yet conquered, they would leave all and never rest till they had gained these treasures.'

Adapting the language of the master catalysts

We have established in this book that the mental monologue that goes through our head creates the emotion that you feel at that point.

Now, we are going to distil the wisdom of the master catalysts into language that we can use on a daily basis.

To attract positive, joyful and prosperous situations to you, you must be that way yourself.

You are not looking for joy—you *are* joy.

If you have an open, loving, positive attitude, anything burdensome in life can be lightened. Happiness isn't some *thing* in the material world that can be acquired and stored and used when needed or wanted.

Joy is accessible when you place an 'I am' statement in your imagination; it will reflect your knowledge that happiness is an inside job. Happiness is an inner belief that you bring to everyone and everything you undertake, rather than expecting your happiness to come to you from others or from your accomplishments and acquisitions.

Therefore, it is important to be aware of your mood. It is created by your thoughts. Train yourself to think this way.

1. All is always well.
2. I am confident and capable.
3. I attract positive people in my life.
4. I know who I am and I am enough.
5. The positive energy around me is continuously expanding.
6. I choose to be present and mindful right now.
7. I am grateful for my miraculous life.
8. I choose to think positive thoughts that serve me.
9. I fulfil the promises I make to myself and others.
10. I love sharing my happiness with everyone around me.
11. I feel energetic and so alive.

12. I am in control of the way I respond to the behaviour of others.
13. I have the will. I have the way.
14. I am love, peace, hope, joy, truth and positive, radiant light!
15. I forgive and release. I am filling my heart and mind with love.
16. All of my needs are met. I thrive from where I am right now.
17. I inhale positivity and exhale negativity.
18. I fuel my body with health and activity.
19. I am talented, creative and successful.
20. Like the waves of an ocean, peace washes over me, cleansing and rejuvenating my spirit.
21. I choose to reach for a better feeling.
22. I grow stronger every day.
23. I speak kindly to myself and others.
24. My life is unfolding perfectly.
25. I choose to see everyone as an opportunity and search for solutions.

State your intention to live a happy, contented life; place it in your now.

In one of the earlier chapters, we discussed some of the common statements people make: 'You never accept your mistakes.'

'Why can't you just admit that you messed up!'

Society considers repeatedly owning up to one's fault as a virtue.

Let me tell you that there's nothing farther from the truth. When circumstances and/or your senses try to influence you that you're wrong, gently allow those thoughts to drift by like passing clouds as you focus on your nourishing imagination, which cannot be altered without your agreement.

Probable responses: 'Let's focus on what can be done today' is a good response to someone who wants you to keep apologizing for your past.

Because if you start believing that you messed up, the past event will continue to threaten your self-esteem. And that's very expensive.

Another important part is the temptation to tell people 'Hey, I'm living by this whole new "I am" philosophy.'

There may be a handful of people who attempt to convince you the 'I am happy' affirmation is totally nuts! Who the hell talks like that?

Precisely! Very few! That's why the income distribution in the world is as skewed as it is!

The athlete who says to himself, 'It's so hot in here' or 'I'm boiling', will perform very differently from the athlete who says, 'Keep pushing, you're doing well'.

Persist in stating your inner mantras of 'I am happy' and 'I am content' while assuming the feeling in your body, in the now.

*False words are not only evil in themselves,
but they infect the soul with evil.*

—SOCRATES

IN CONCLUSION

15

Awaken the Voice Within You

When we want to improve ourselves in some way, we are not just competing with our old programming; we are competing with the requirements of daily living.

It is important to understand this—go back to the chapter on 'motivation'.

Making changes on the inside is seldom easy. When we decide to change, we are suddenly confronted with a wall of hurdles that we had not prepared for.

You need all five values—honesty, diligence, fire, passion and agile-mindedness to be able to complete the process.

If you improve *who* you are, by that same law, you will improve your life.

The more successful you become *inside,* the more successes you will automatically create on the outside.

Each of us has three resources which allow us to get through any given day.

1. The number of hours in a day.
2. Our priorities for the day.
3. The energy we have to live that day.

Our desire to improve ourselves competes for resources with all of the above.

We have our profession, our personal duties and our own biological needs to take care of, every day. There are things to think about, so many small and big decisions to make, things to figure out, problems to solve, things to consider, understand and deal with. In the middle of all this, we have to find time to rewire and adopt the THECO mindset. Sometimes, most days for some of us, there is just no energy left.

Our desire to improve ourselves competes with the demands which we or others have placed on us emotionally. We are too busy existing to really live.

Because you can't improve if you cannot keep your eyes open. You are trying to create a new habit of positive mental monologues, and new routines that will serve you.

Remember, you cannot make all the transformation you want in one day. So don't go crazy.

Here's a good way to start.

1. Attach your new habit to an existing old habit. For example, smile and say nice things to yourself when you brush every morning.
2. Make a small change, like waking up each morning 10 minutes earlier, and write something you would like to accomplish that day. This is better than saying 'from tomorrow, I'm a 4 a.m. dude'. When the change is drastic, there is high resistance.
3. Create a peer group that will make you accountable for doing stuff, like a running group or an exercise group. If the value you're working on is discipline, and the mental monologue you're giving yourself is that 'you're a go-getter', being part of a peer group

will make it that much more difficult to bow out.

You can also build a reward system into the process so you can take time to celebrate the successful completion of your goals. The reward you pick is up to you, but it's important to celebrate those big moments along the way.

There are simple ways to keep yourself on the path to self-transformation.

Imagine that we begin these precepts in school and teach our children the value of incremental change.

We could then raise a generation of children for whom depression and disease are alien concepts.

This would be nation building of another kind altogether!

The emotional victory of 6 a.m.

Have you ever thought about why getting up at 6 a.m., or 5 a.m. is a big deal?

You will encounter many people who will say that 'I am not a morning person'. Of course you aren't if you say that to yourself!

There will be those who even argue with you—I cannot sleep before 12 in the night; I get all my work done in the night; I don't see the point in being a morning person.

Here's the big deal about getting up at 6 a.m. or 5 a.m. or 4 a.m.

It's a psychological separator; of you versus them.

Staying up late is easy.

Getting up early, consistently, requires doing. It's not just vanity.

Because when you 'start' doing something that less than 1 per cent of the world is capable of doing, then you automatically extend it to other spheres of your life.

You believe that you're capable of doing what others can't. And like colour spreads on wet paper, the idea of you being 'capable' permeates every fibre of the way you treat yourself.

It changes the way you talk to yourself. Your mental monologue becomes, 'I am capable', 'I am disciplined'.

This is validated when all around you, you begin to observe that people are barely making it to work on time, dishevelled and rushing from meeting to meeting, unplanned and clueless because they did not rise early, generate 'me' time to establish their day's priorities, and take time out to plan their day.

Bullet points of how to rescript your life

Our inner talk is almost constant and so habituated that most of the time we don't even notice it.

We often don't try to create this inner talk; it just happens on autopilot. It can happen so quickly that just one thought leads to an almost instantaneous stream of related thoughts. Since the majority of our self-talk is negative, it creates a lens through which we view the world.

The first step towards freedom from self-talk is to recognize we have a voice in our heads; the second step is to observe what the voice is saying.

Here is a summary of ways outlined in this book to master your mental monologue:

- The feelings and emotions produced by our inner talk lead to bodily reactions such as those associated with anxiety, stress or depression.
- We don't even realize the damage we do to ourselves. Our worst enemy lies between our ears and causes

unhealthy behavioural manifestations on a daily basis. Consciously deserve your self-dialogue and change any thought or statement that doesn't serve you.
- Always speak to yourself in the present tense—you want to achieve your goal now, not in some indefinable future. For example, if your goal is to find a job, don't say, 'I will have a job', using the future tense. Say, 'I have a well-paying and wonderful job, which I love and enjoy'. Simply *wanting* to attract more prosperity into your life, and saying 'I will be rich someday' is equivalent to telling your brain that 'I am not rich today'. 'I am not' projects a state of lack. This is the programme you fit into your brain.
- Be specific. Tell your mind exactly what it is that you want—in the present tense.
- Remember that your internal monologue is a private matter between you and your source of being. Inviting others to support or consider your intentions is an invitation to responses. These may try to tell you that your intention is crazy and vacuous. You'll be tempted to defend your stand or to explain yourself. This will shift your inner intentions. You will move from emotion to logic, imagination to reasoning. And both are limiting choices.
- Manifestation of the effects of your positive affirmative mental monologue is a deeply spiritual exercise. Thus, it defies all sorts of objective opinions.
- Attach strong feelings and desires to your monologue with yourself. You should feel and believe that what you are saying is already true. Feelings and emotions give life to your words.

- Positive thoughts attract other positive thoughts, and negative thoughts attract other negative thoughts. Positive thinking alone is not enough. You have to act on your thoughts—defeat your old autopilot—for them to work.
- Remember that you will become what you believe in, not what you want. And this is the core truth you need to understand and internalize.

Here's to peaceable future for our planet.

He who has realized eternal Truth does not see death, nor illness, nor pain; he sees everything as the self, and obtains all.

—CHANDOGYA UPANISHAD

Epilogue

So who am I today?

What qualifies me to give you this advice?

I am inspired.

I am the product of thousands of years of consciousness that is flowing through me today as I write to you.

In fact, this manuscript that has stayed with me for four years now refuses to stay with me anymore.

I have survived a near-death experience. I have survived intense emotional trauma.

Like you, I have cried in the bus back home, felt like giving up one day and deleted phone numbers of people who I felt were mean to me.

Like you, I have believed that I could let others hurt me without my permission.

Like you, I felt that some day will be mine, maybe not today. And I have postponed my joy by one more day.

Like you, on some days, I have tried to explain why I feel so positive, and got into a silly argument that defeated the purpose of my positivity.

Like you, I have felt envy, disappointment and fear. And made tonnes of mistakes.

And yet, one day, I reached a tipping point.

I started loving myself.

Others followed suit.

I said a big, resounding yes to myself.

I feel zero degree of separation with any other human being in the world.

I am beyond me, and one with the universe.

As are you!

Bibliography

Arnold, E.V. *The Rigveda,* 1960, reprinted 1972.
Cain, Susan. *Quiet: The Power of Introverts in a World That Can't Stop Talking,* Broadway Books, 2011.
Majumdar, R.C. *The Vedic Age,* 1951, reprinted 1957.
Mitchell, Kevin. *The Future of the Brain: Essays by the World's Leading Neuroscientists,* Princeton University Press, 2014.
Olivelle, P. tr. *Samnyāsa Upanishads,* 1992.
Pandit Satyakam Vidyalankar. *The Holy Vedas: A Golden Treasury,* Delhi, Clarion Books, 1983.
Ramanan K.V. *Nagarjuna's Philosophy* (New Edition), Motilal Banarsidass, 2016.
Reardon, Sara. 'The Human Connectome Project', *Nature,* 28 September 2015.
Sinek, Simon. *Start With Why: How Great Leaders Inspire Everyone to Take Action,* Portfolio, Penguin, 2011.
Swamini Atmaprajnananda. *Nomenclature of the Vedas,* D. K. Printworld, First edition, 2012.
Tolle, Eckhart. *The Power of Now: A Guide to Spiritual Enlightenment,* Yogi Impressions Books, 2006.
Winternitz, M. *History of Indian Literature,* 3 Vol., tr. 1927–33.
Yogi Ramacharaka. *The Spirit of the Upanishads,* The Yogi Publication Society, Chicago, 1907.

www.ingramcontent.com/pod-product-compliance
Lightning Source LLC
Chambersburg PA
CBHW050907160426
43194CB00011B/2317